The Dominican Republic

THE DOMINICAN REPUBLIC
Politics and Development in an Unsovereign State

JAN KNIPPERS BLACK
University of New Mexico

Boston
ALLEN & UNWIN
London Sydney

Copyright © 1986 by Allen & Unwin, Inc.
All rights reserved.

Allen & Unwin, Inc.
8 Winchester Place, Winchester, MA 01890, USA

George Allen & Unwin (Publishers) Ltd,
40 Museum Street, London WC1A 1LU, UK

George Allen & Unwin (Publishers) Ltd,
Park Lane, Hemel Hempstead, Herts HP2 4TE, UK

George Allen & Unwin Australia Pty Ltd,
8 Napier Street, North Sydney, NSW 2060, Australia

First Published in 1986

Library of Congress Cataloging-in-Publication Data

Black, Jan Knippers, 1940–
  The Dominican Republic.

  Bibliography: p.
  Includes index.
  1. Dominican Republic—Politics and government.
I. Title.
F1938.B55   1986   972.93   86-1219
ISBN 0-04-497000-5 (alk. paper)
ISBN 0-04-497001-3 (pbk. : alk. paper)

British Library Cataloguing in Publication Data

Black, Jan Knippers
  The Dominican Republic : politics and
  development in an unsovereign state.
  1. Dominican Republic—History
I. Title
972.93   F1938
ISBN 0-04-497000-5
ISBN 0-04-497001-3 Pbk)

972.93 B627d

Black, Jan Knippers, 1940–

The Dominican Republic

TO
*John II and Marc Black,
Steve and Dan Needler,
and Mary Marfise*

CONTENTS

Preface xi

1
INTRODUCTION: PERSPECTIVES ON DOMINICAN POLITICS

"The Land Columbus Loved Best" 3
The Dependent State 7
The Company State 8
The Developing State 10

2
HISTORICAL BACKGROUND

Conquest: The End and the Beginning 13
The Colony 15
Haitian Occupation (1822–1844) 17
Uncertain Nationhood (1844–1916) 19
Occupation by the United States (1916–1924) 21
The Era of Trujillo 25

3
CONTEMPORARY HISTORY

A Botched Palace Coup 29
A Short-Lived Democracy 31
An Abortive Revolution 36

A Suspect Election	39
Trujillismo without Trujillo: The Rule of Balaguer	42
A Pivotal Election	52

4
SOCIAL AND ECONOMIC STRUCTURES

Race and Social Stratification	55
Demographic Trends	61
Economic Growth and Diversification	62
Dependency and Development	66
A Tale of Deprivation and of Hope	70

5
POLITICAL INSTITUTIONS

The Structure of Government	75
The Contemporary Party System	81

6
SOCIAL SECTORS AND INTEREST GROUPS

The Economic Elite	93
Organized Labor	95
Peasant Movements	98
The Roman Catholic Church	98
Students	101
The Armed Forces	102

7
THE DOMINICAN REPUBLIC IN INTERNATIONAL POLITICS

Domestic Correlates of Foreign Policy	110
Relations with the United States	113
Relations with Haiti	119
Cautiously Expanding Horizons	122

8
THE NEW ERA OF PRD RULE: POLICIES AND POLITICS

The Presidency of Guzmán	129
The Rule of Jorge Blanco and the International Monetary Fund	138

9
CONCLUSION

Passing the Mantle	147
A Family Affair	148
The Best of Times, the Worst of Times	149

Bibliography 151

Index 159

PREFACE

This book is really two in one. It is scarcely possible in a brief and general study such as this one to convey to the reader a sense of the richness of texture, of the villainy and heroism, the pathos and intrigue and high drama that characterize Dominican politics. The reader approaching the subject for the first time may not wish to be burdened with excessive detail, much less with rumor or with conflicting accounts of the same event. Thus the text provides generalizations and a fairly straightforward account of circumstances and events that can be confirmed with some degree of confidence. However, for the specialist—in search of new tidbits of information or new controversies to resolve—and for the devotee of mystery and intrigue, the fun is in the footnotes.

I acknowledge with gratitude the assistance of a Mellon Inter-American Field Research Grant awarded by the Latin American Institute of the University of New Mexico. I am also grateful to the many Dominicans who were helpful to me in my research, particularly Alfonso Moreno Martínez, Guido D'Alessandro, and Ramón Martínez-Portorreal.

1

INTRODUCTION:
PERSPECTIVES ON DOMINICAN POLITICS

In general, the Dominican Republic has intruded into the consciousness of Americans and other foreigners only when Americans or other foreigners have intruded into the territory or the affairs of that small country. The republic merits more constant and inclusive attention, however, from scholars and others, not only because it is unique and intrinsically interesting, but also because it is a potential source of insight into problems facing many other countries, especially those of Latin America and the Caribbean. The experience of the Dominican Republic offers particularly provocative insight into the nature and consequences of unequal relations among states.

The island of Hispaniola, which the Dominican Republic shares with Haiti, lies to the south and east of Cuba, west of Puerto Rico. After Cuba, it is the largest island of the West Indian archipelago. Occupying the eastern two-thirds of the island, the republic is small in global terms, but larger than all other Caribbean island states except Cuba. The approximately 19,000 square miles of the Dominican Republic encompass a variety of ecological zones, from cool mountains to tepid plains and from tropical rain forests to scorching desert to balmy beaches. Its population is small but fast-growing, having more than doubled from 3 million in 1960 to more than 6 million in the mid 1980s. Its people, for the most part, are miserably poor, but the land is rich, capable of producing a great variety of tropical and temperate crops, as well as containing such mineral deposits as bauxite, nickel, and gold in commercial quantities. The country is underdeveloped, with much of its human and material potential unrealized, but it is rapidly moderniz-

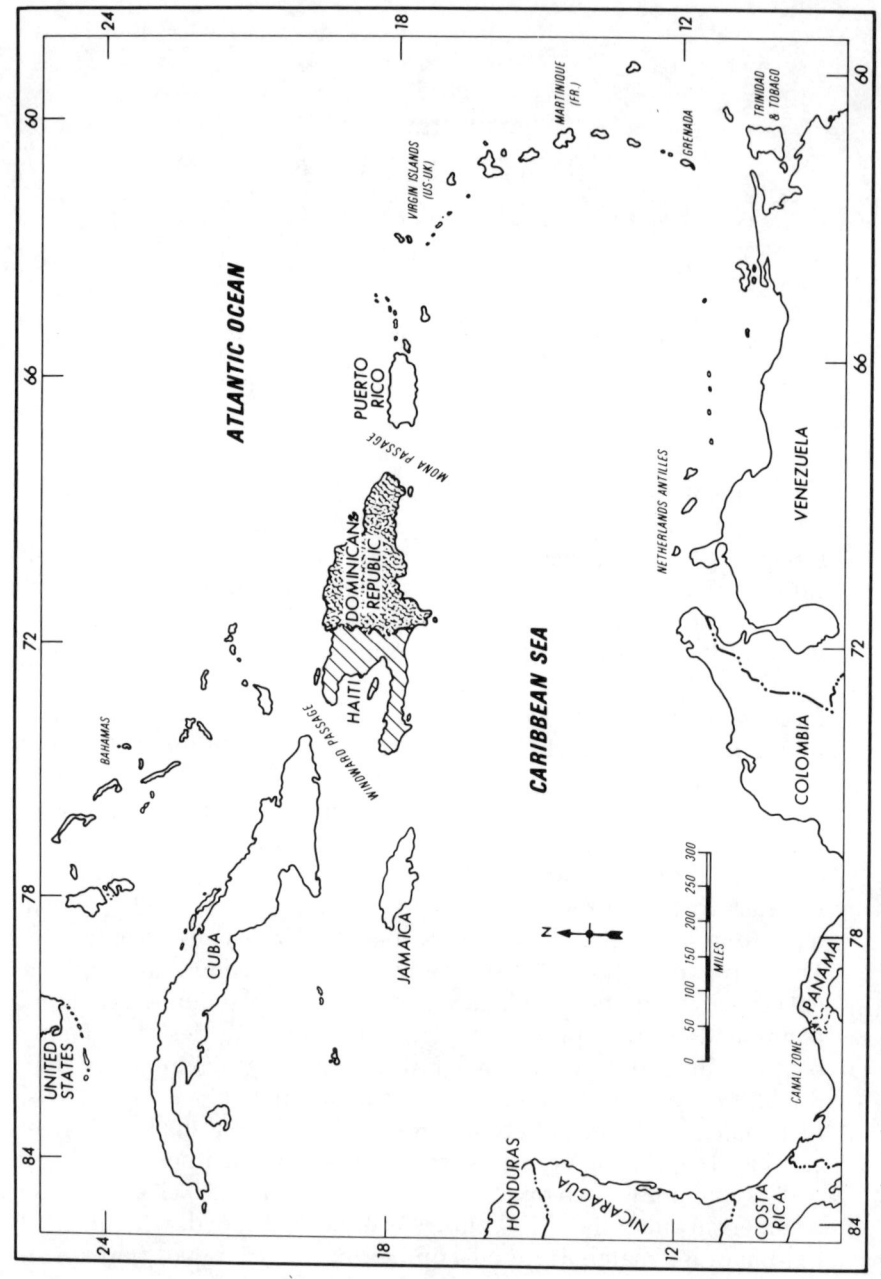

Hispaniola and its position in the Antilles.

1. INTRODUCTION: PERSPECTIVES ON DOMINICAN POLITICS

ing under the prod of governments and foreign investors. Subsistence agriculture has gradually given way, for example, to agribusiness—especially sugar production—for export. The republic has exercised little influence in regional or world affairs, but has often been a victim of the fears and ambitions of other states. The political elite, as a consequence, in part, of its insecurity and of frequent stints in exile, is surprisingly cosmopolitan.

Socially and culturally, the republic represents a blend of Latin America and Caribbean characteristics or, one might say, of Spanish and African influences. The population is predominantly mulatto, with little remaining trace of the pre-Colombian indigenous peoples. Spanish is spoken universally and Roman Catholicism is practiced almost universally, although Protestant missionaries have made inroads and some elements of African religions have persisted or have been reintroduced from Haiti. While the republic differs in some respects from the norms both of Latin America and of the Caribbean, it is well positioned to serve as a cultural bridge between the two regions.

This book focuses on Dominican politics—that is, on the competition for power—in its broadest sense and on the relationship between politics and social and economic development. There are many possible ways of viewing that competitive process, its actors and issues and outcomes and the ways in which it has influenced and drawn upon other aspects of the national experience. It cannot be separated from the ways in which Dominicans see themselves and are seen by others. To a large extent, what the observer stands to learn about, and from, the republic depends on the perspective employed. A few such perspectives are suggested below.

"The Land Columbus Loved Best"

Commenting on the promotional theme of the tourist industry, a visitor to Santo Domingo was heard to quip that if Columbus loved the Dominican Republic best, it must have been because of all the great Italian restaurants. A backwater town just two decades ago, Santo Domingo has blossomed, with the tourist trade, into a highly cosmopolitan and vibrant city.

The concerted effort on the part of the government and domestic and foreign enterprises to develop the country's potential for attracting and accommodating tourists is a relatively recent phenomenon. The potential, however, has always been there. Physically, the Dominican Republic is a land of striking contrasts and pristine beauty. Its historical monuments denote its significance as a cradle of Spanish colonial rule in the New World and as a staging area for further conquest. And its culture is one of spontaneity, creativity, and good-natured humor.

Within the past decade, tourist enclaves have proliferated along both the northern and southern coasts. The ancient port town of Puerto Plata has been refurbished and restored as a tourist attraction and the center of the tourist trade on the north coast. Resorts in that area cater to the middle-class tourist, from Europe as well as from the United States and Canada. There the hedonist may bask on palm-fringed sandy beaches, or bathe in warm emerald waters and snorkel along the coral reefs amid the multicolored fish. But the hardier traveler will go in search of beaches as yet undeveloped and will explore the country's multifaceted interior.

Most of the national terrain is rugged and mountainous, with peaks towering above 10,000 feet. The mountains, cloaked in luxuriant green, are divided into four parallel ranges, extending in a northwesterly direction in the western part of the country, and a single low range extending east to west in the eastern part of the island. Transportation across the steep slopes and yawning canyons of the highlands can be precarious, and settlement at higher altitudes is sparse.

Population is heaviest around Santo Domingo on the southern shore and in the broad and fertile Cibao Valley that extends along a northwest–southeast axis between the major mountain ranges in the northern half of the country. Centrally situated in the valley, on the Yaque del Norte River, is the historic city of Santiago, the country's second largest, with a population of 400,000. Once aristocratic, culture conscious, and serene, it now exhibits on a smaller scale the commercial bedlam of Santo Domingo. To the east of Santiago, the valley is known as the *Vega Real*, or Royal Plain, an alluvial flood plain of rich and deep topsoil, planted in grains and tobacco.

Proceeding toward the southwest, the valleys become more arid and rocky, scarcely hospitable to the subsistence farmers who eke out a living there. The southernmost Neiba Valley contains the country's largest natural lake, formerly part of a strait, whose waters plunge to 140 feet below sea level.

The Caribbean Coastal Plain, covering more than a thousand square miles of the easternmost part of the island, is the area best suited to sugarcane production. Much of the plain was owned for almost two

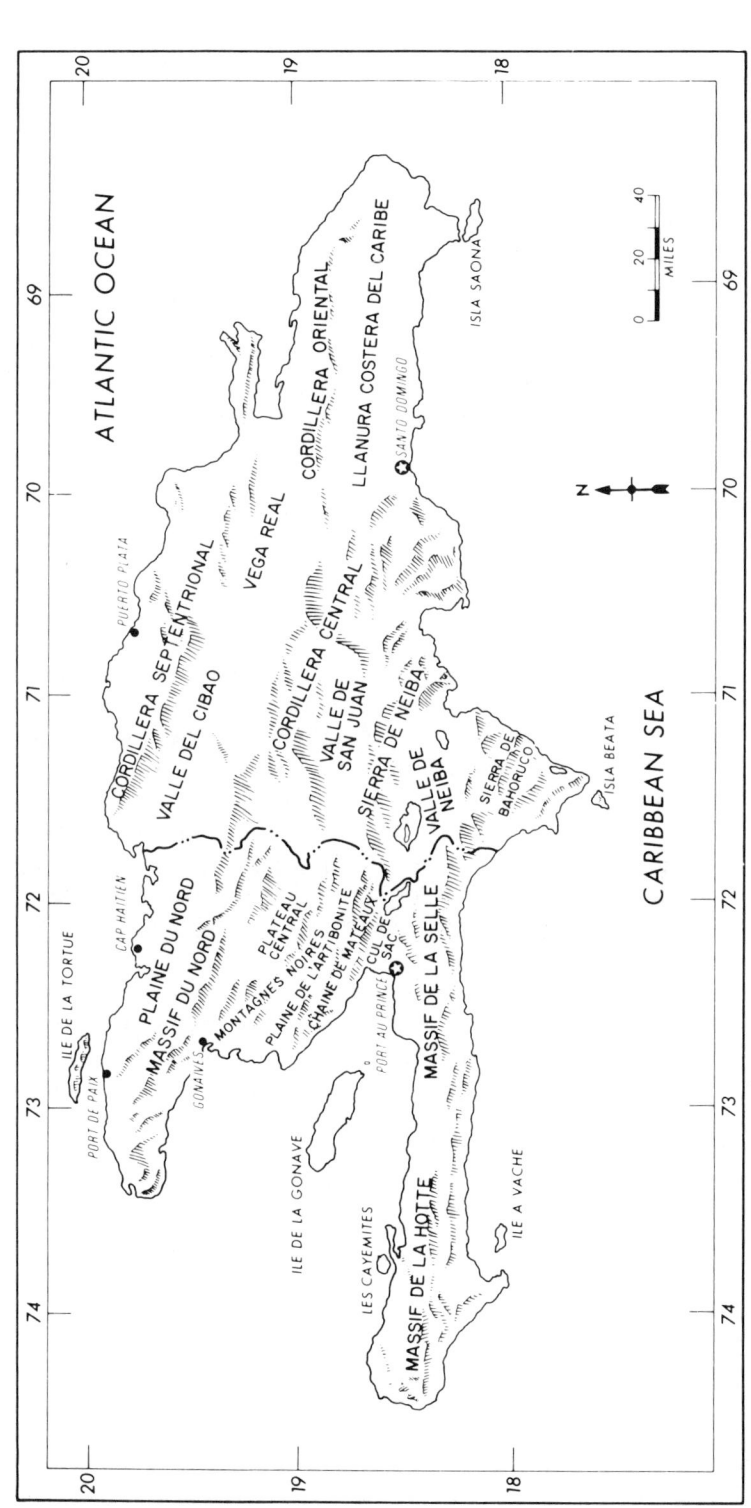

Relief features of Hispaniola.

decades by the U.S.-based Gulf and Western Corporation; Gulf and Western lands and assets were purchased in January 1985 by a group of investors headed by the Fanjul brothers of Florida. La Romana, site of the country's largest sugar refinery, is a company town, relatively modern and thriving and essentially off-limits to Dominican labor and political organizers. It is also the center of tourism on the southern coast.

The Casa de Campo complex, also purchased by the Fanjul group from Gulf and Western, consists of three hotels, a complex of villas, a model sixteenth-century Spanish village, two golf courses, a polo field, swimming pools, tennis courts, and other facilities, including its own airport. The well-heeled tourist can land virtually on the private beach and ignore entirely the rest of the country. The less affluent and more adventurous beachcombers might like to explore the lovely but less developed beaches around Guayacanes or mix with multitudes of Dominicans at the Boca Chica beach, nearer the capital.

Santo Domingo, in addition to being the country's political, financial, and commercial center, is also one of its major tourist attractions. There the Spanish Crown established its first administrative center. The graceful palace Alcázar de Colón, built by Columbus's son, Diego, still stands on the ramparts of the old city, where homes and shops along narrow, cobblestone streets have been restored in colonial style. The New World's oldest cathedral guards the remains of Christopher Columbus. The Museo del Hombre Dominicano (Museum of Dominican Man), in the modern Plaza de la Cultura, traces the country's social history from the conquest and destruction of the indigenous Tainos to the present.

Known as the "cradle of America" in the early colonial period, the colony was the center from which European civilization spread to the New World. It had the first schools and convents in America; and literature, theater, architecture, and other arts flourished. Since the mid sixteenth century, deprivation and war, anarchy and tyranny have taken their toll, and the arts have never fully recovered the place in Dominican society they once enjoyed. Nevertheless, for the visitor, there is much to see and do and enjoy. The devotee of popular culture will want to dance the *merenque*, and to listen to folk music, in vogue since the 1960s, or to the untrained but inventive street musicians who ply their trade along the Malecon, or coastal boulevard. The sports fan will take in a cock fight or a baseball game. For the higher brows, there are concerts and art galleries, museums and libraries.

1. INTRODUCTION: PERSPECTIVES ON DOMINICAN POLITICS

An interest in Dominican culture would quickly lead the visitor into the political sphere because "the new wave" *(la nueva ola)* in literature and the arts was born in the late 1960s as a search for new means of expressing social protest. Such expression has been notable, for example, in folklore, political irony and satire, and paintings and murals charged with social content.

Less inquisitive tourists may confine themselves to their beach enclaves and remain oblivious to the travails of Dominican politics. But tourism, as a development scheme, a source of foreign exchange, and a lure for foreign investment, has in itself become a highly politicized issue. Many Dominicans see tourism as the most promising potential replacement for the failing sugar industry as the country's primary foreign-exchange earner.

Some civilian political leaders see in tourism a special noneconomic bonus; they believe it offers a modicum of insurance for the constitutional system. As tourists tend to shy away from countries experiencing civil turmoil or military rule, these politicians believe that an emphasis on tourism will give party leaders greater incentive to resolve their differences without resort to agitation in the streets. They also believe that tourism will give leaders of the business community, domestic and foreign, an unaccustomed dread of military intervention and a predilection to support the constitutional system.

The Dependent State

Many modern nation-states have had to fight for their independence, but the Dominicans have had to fight repeatedly for theirs. Just as there have always been some among them who were willing to relinquish sovereignty for protection or to sell out the national patrimony for personal or factional advantage, there have been many others willing to risk everything to retrieve or secure independence for their small state. The very precariousness of independence and the experience of fighting for it from generation to generation have contributed a certain poignancy and intensity to Dominican nationalism.

Throughout the nineteenth century, before, during, and after the period when most Latin American states were winning their independence, Dominican territory seemed to be up for grabs. After attempting to control the entire island of Hispaniola for 200 years, the Spanish ceded the western third—now Haiti—to France. After another 100 years, it ceded the other two-thirds—now the Dominican Republic—to France as well. At the turn of the nineteenth century, a slave revolt in the west spilled over, and for several years Haitian, French, and Spanish armies fought for control over the entire island. With British help, the Spanish regained control of the eastern colony in 1809. The Dominicans declared their independence from Spain in 1821 only to be overrun a year later by the Haitians.

The Haitians were expelled in 1844, but independence was to be short-lived, as the Spanish returned, invited by the republic's ruling general in 1861. The Spanish were expelled for the last time in 1865. By that time, however, the well-trampled territory had attracted the covetous attention of the United States. The U.S. president Ulysses S. Grant, in negotiation with another Dominican general, considered annexing the republic.

Annexation was not to be, but by the turn of the century, the indebted country had fallen under U.S. suzerainty, demonstrated first by the establishment of a customs receivership and from 1916 to 1924 by outright military occupation and martial law. The Dominican economy and the Dominican military, reconstructed during the occupation, thus became tightly linked to the United States.

Since the first U.S. occupation, Dominican independence has been qualified by the country's dependence on U.S. markets and on U.S. public aid and private investment. It has been qualified, in particular, by the dependence of the Dominican armed forces on their U.S. counterparts and by the continued willingness of the United States to intervene militarily, if necessary, to impose its will. The point was made in no uncertain terms by the U.S. marine invasion and occupation of 1965–1966.

Intervention by the United States has not always been unwelcome. The Carter administration's diplomatic support for the electoral process in 1978 was well received. Nevertheless, the nation's relationship of subordination to the United States is a source of widespread and deep-seated resentment and a factor that must be included in any analysis of political actions and policy options.

The Company State

Because of the overwhelming role of the U.S.-based Gulf and Western Corporation in the Dominican economy since the mid 1960s, the

1. INTRODUCTION: PERSPECTIVES ON DOMINICAN POLITICS

republic has sometimes been called a company state. All the major private sectors of the economy—agro-industry, mining, tourism, and light manufacturing—are controlled by foreign, mainly U.S., companies. Some 125 subsidiaries of U.S. firms were operating in the country in the mid 1980s, and total U.S. private investment was estimated at some $500 million. But the investments and activities of Gulf and Western were of such magnitude as to dwarf those of other companies.

With investments totaling more than $200 million, Gulf and Western was the country's largest private landowner, employer, and exporter. It owned almost half of the country's best sugar-producing land and the largest sugar mill, and it produced about one-third of the country's sugar. In addition to sugar, Gulf and Western exported tobacco, meat, and citrus fruits. The company also had a large and expanding role in the republic's food-processing, cement, construction, and tourist industries, as well as in real estate and finance.

With its sugarcane fields, its mill and related industries at La Romana, its extensive and self-contained tourist enclaves of Casa de Campo and Altos de Chavon, and its huge industrial park, Gulf and Western had virtually undisputed control of the easternmost portion of the island. Gulf and Western operated the industrial park under a 30-year, tax-free contract with the government. About one-fourth of the companies operating in the park's industrial free zone were Gulf and Western subsidiaries.

The company's influence was such that the Dominican government usually gave Gulf and Western preferential access to the best-paying and most reliable sugar markets, at the expense of state-owned sugar-producing operations.[1] A revolving door at the upper levels of company and government administration allowed former company managers to serve in important government posts and former government officials to move into company management. Kinship ties also enhanced the company's access to government. But the influence that the company wielded was based not only on its preponderant role in the Dominican economy and the direct links it had established to the Dominican government; it also flowed from the influence the company enjoyed with the U.S. government. In the early 1980s Gulf and Western was the sixty-first-largest corporate conglomerate in the United

---

1. Tom Barry, Beth Wood, and Deb Preusch, *The Other Side of Paradise: Foreign Control in the Caribbean* (New York: Grove Press, 1984), pp. 289–304.

States, with annual sales amounting to more than the Dominican Republic's gross national product.

Gulf and Western and its defenders in the Dominican Republic argued that the company provided essential capital and jobs and deserved much of the credit for the country's economic growth and modernization within the last two decades. Its detractors countered that the company paid too little in wages and taxes; that it bought out or squeezed out local businesses and discouraged local initiative; that it crushed unions and corrupted governments; and, finally, that the company, in concert with the U.S. government, cast a long shadow over Dominican sovereignty.

Regardless of the attitudes and actions of any particular Dominican government, the status of Gulf and Western was always a major issue in Dominican politics. Thus, the company's decision, first announced in June 1984, to unload its Dominican properties came as a shock to most Dominicans. For Dominican nationalists, it was scarcely cause for celebration. With the Fanjul group, which took over control of most of Gulf and Western's major holdings in early 1985, the republic remained a company state, but the new company was an unknown entity, and the nature of its influence over Dominican economic and political systems remained to be seen.

The Developing State

Though progress has come in spurts, interspersed with periods of stagnation or decline, it is clear that the republic has made great strides in the last two decades in economic growth and modernization. Development, however, is a subjective concept; the country's progress in that regard is less readily measured. To most observers, including most politically articulate Dominicans, development means a great deal more than technological borrowing or national aggregate figures on a balance sheet. It means equity as well as accumulation, choices and opportunity as well as occupation and sustenance, a sense of self-worth and dignity as well as national pride, and some degree of control over personal and national destinies.

Among the more specific development goals articulated by the republic's popularly elected presidents since 1978 have been rural resettlement and technical assistance to small farmers so as to increase domestic food production, raise rural incomes, and slow the pace of

1. INTRODUCTION: PERSPECTIVES ON DOMINICAN POLITICS

migration to the cities; diversification of economic activities and export industries so as to make the economy less vulnerable to price fluctuations in world markets, particularly for sugar; attraction of foreign capital so as to accelerate the creation of jobs, but under conditions that preserve a measure of local control; the further exploitation of hydroelectric power and the search for other domestic sources of energy; and the expansion of social services and welfare programs. The more ambitious and more nearly revolutionary goals erected by the ruling Dominican Revolutionary party (Partido Revolucionario Dominicano—PRD) in the early 1960s have not been abandoned entirely, but they have been set aside for pursuit on a sunnier day.

Contemporary PRD governments have had some notable successes. The republic has become self-sufficient—at least during some years—in the production of its staple foods, rice and beans. Progress has been made in the promotion of tourism and in the construction of physical and institutional infrastructure to support new industries. Gold, from a mine owned by the state, has become an important addition to the export list. Several hundred new clinics and schools have been built, and literacy and vocational education programs have been promoted.

Nevertheless, progress in most areas has been meager at best. Many urgent problems have remained unattended, have resisted governmental solution, or have been aggravated by the recession that set in in the late 1970s. Many government agencies and enterprises are virtually bankrupt, and new clinics and schools lack medicines and books. Deprivation and despair in the countryside, and in some areas the encroachment of agribusiness, continue to push peasants into the unwelcoming city. Even before the recession hit, the creation of new jobs in industry was failing to keep pace with the appearance of new job seekers. Whereas in 1970 there were 7 jobs in industry for each 100 urban dwellers, by 1977 there were only 5 jobs per 100.[2]

Rising prices for imports, especially petroleum, falling prices for exports, and the consequent urgent need for more foreign credit, in the face of servicing requirements for an already enormous foreign debt, have left the country in a chronic economic crisis. The International Monetary Fund's (IMF) austerity solution, which there as elsewhere in the Third World has been the price of keeping credit lines open, has meant cuts in wages and social services and increases in prices and

---

2. *Ibid.*

working hours. As usual, most new hardships have been borne by the working and would-be-working classes rather than by the affluent.

The most promising aspects of development in the Dominican Republic within the last two decades have been in the political sphere rather than in the economic one. Those decades have seen tyranny and anarchy, military intervention, civilian uprising, U.S. occupation, and government-sanctioned terror, but they have also seen the development of a modern political party, of the seeds of a labor movement, of organization among women, students, and others who presume to speak for the traditionally disadvantaged, and of new approaches to cooperation at the community level.

Those decades have seen the beginnings of universal adult franchise and free elections. The period since 1978 has also seen progress in the subordination of the military to civilian authority and in the expectation that decisions of the electorate will be honored. The system remains fragile, and politically astute Dominicans tread lightly on the interests of traditional power brokers; but as long as the system remains relatively open and democratic there remains hope for progress toward development in its fuller sense—of the self-realization of all Dominicans.

2
HISTORICAL BACKGROUND

Conquest: The End and the Beginning

The pathos that must tinge all accounts of Dominican history begins at the beginning. Little is known of the indigenous peoples of the island Columbus named Hispaniola. But such accounts as exist suggest that the numerically dominant group, the Tainos, were gentle and generous—utterly undeserving of the fate they were to suffer at the hands of the Spaniards.

The Tainos were of the language group known as *Arawak*, meaning "meal" or "cassava eater". The main element in their diet was yucca, though they also cultivated sweet potatoes, chilis, peanuts, and corn; and they caught fish, shellfish, turtles, and manatee. They fished with wooden spears from dugout canoes. Implements for farming and building were relatively primitive: sharpened sticks and ax heads of polished stone.

Subsequent generations of Hispanics were to notice that the Tainos had been highly skilled in sculpture, ceramics, and basket weaving. But Columbus and his men scarcely took note of such unshiny things, as they were distracted by the natives' adornments of gold. Gold was worked in this late Neolithic culture solely for purposes of adornment—masks, for example, and necklaces. Such adornment was, in fact, about the only kind Tainos of either sex used; they wore no clothes.

The Tainos called their island Haiti, but they also called a part of it Quisqueya—a name contemporary Dominicans sometimes use to refer to their country. The Tainos had divided the island into five provinces, each having its own *cacique*, or chief. Land was owned and worked communally. At the time of discovery, there was little or no warfare among Taino villages. There was, however, in the eastern part of the island, around Samaná Bay, a settlement of Caribs. This warlike and cannibalistic people preyed on the Tainos and, with their bows and arrows, resisted the incursions of the Europeans.

Columbus recorded in the logbook of his first voyage that the Taino were a "very open-hearted people, who give what they are asked for with the best will in the world and, when asked, seem to regard themselves as having been greatly honored by the request." He also said, "They bear no arms, and are all so unprotected and so very cowardly that a thousand would not face three; so they are fit to be ordered about and made to work. . . ."[1]

On Christmas Day, 1492, Columbus's flagship, the *Santa María*, ran aground in the vicinity of what is now Cap Haitien, in Haiti. Columbus named the place Natividad, and as a friendly cacique offered hospitality there, left a colony of 39 men. Returning the following year, on his second voyage, he found no colony. The Spaniards, abusing the hospitality of the Tainos, had gone about in search of gold and women. A less tolerant cacique, who found the Spaniards holding five captured women apiece, drove them into the sea.

Rumors among the Taino of gold to the east in the Cibao Valley region led Columbus and his men to establish a second colony there in 1494. At Isabela, the settlers planted melons, wheat, and sugarcane, but most of their energy was devoted to the pursuit of gold. While Columbus explored the coastline to the south, his men raped and plundered and captured slaves for shipment back to Spain. He returned to find Spaniards and Tainos at war.

By 1496, the surviving Tainos had been subdued and subjected to impossible tributes, mainly from the declining supplies of gold nuggets. Some fled to the high mountains, but thousands killed themselves by taking cassava poison. Many thousands more died of disease and overexertion.

The last Taino rebellion began about 1520 and lasted until 1533. Its leader, Enrique, had been raised and educated by the Spaniards. When he found that both he and his wife were expected to satisfy the whims of a Spanish landlord, Enrique fled to the Bohoruco Mountains near Barahona. There he was joined by a thousand or more of his

1. Seldon Rodman, *Quisqueya: A History of the Dominican Republic* (Seattle: University of Washington Press, 1964), p. 4.

tribesmen. The legend of these rebels, who held a more powerful enemy at bay for 13 years and never surrendered, was recorded by Manuel de Jesus Galván in 1882 in *Enriquillo*, generally considered the country's greatest novel. The war was concluded by a formal peace treaty whereby the remaining Tainos were settled on a reservation. Nevertheless, by the 1550s, the Taino population, estimated at from 1 to 3 million a half century earlier, had virtually disappeared.

Too late, the native peoples of the New World had acquired an effective spokesman. Bartolomé de las Casas accompanied Columbus on his third voyage in 1498 and returned to Hispaniola 4 years later with Don Nicolás de Ovando, who had been appointed governor of all the Indies. In 1510 Las Casas became the first priest ordained in the American colonies. His *History of the Indies*, written in the mid sixteenth century, documented the abuses he had observed in Hispaniola and Cuba and launched a great philosophical debate, in the Old World as well as the New, as to whether or not the indigenous people of the Americas had "souls."

It was finally concluded that the Christianizing mission assumed by the Crown and the church implied recognition of full human status. By that time, however, the indigenous population throughout the New World had been reduced to a small fraction of its former size. Furthermore, African slaves were already being imported to replace the expiring native Americans, and the question of "souls" had been raised again with respect to them.

The Colony

The earliest Spanish settlers in Hispaniola did not fare much better than the indigenous peoples they used and abused. Many hundreds of Spaniards were killed in battles with the Indians, or among themselves, or died of disease or deprivation. But their numbers were continually replenished by new arrivals from the mother country.

The settlement at Isabela was to be short-lived. After the Tainos had been defeated and enslaved, Columbus returned to Spain, leaving his brother Bartolomeo in charge of the colony. As the colonists soon began to fight among themselves, Bartolomeo established a new settlement on the south coast in 1496, taking most of the population of La Isabela with him. The new settlement, on the Ozama River, was later named Santo Domingo. Its population in 1498 was about 300.

Some 2500 settlers arrived with the new governor, Ovando, in 1502, but about half of them died within a few years. Santo Domingo was destroyed by a hurricane during Ovando's governorship, but by the time he left in 1509 the old city, as it stands today, had begun to take shape.

The golden era of the colony of Hispaniola and the city of Santo Domingo came and went early in the 300-year colonial period. It arrived, more or less, with the rule of Christopher Columbus's eldest son, Diego. Diego served as governor of Hispaniola from 1509 to 1515 and as viceroy of the Indies from 1520 to 1524. Having married into Spanish aristocracy, Diego built a beautiful palace, the Alcázar—which still stands—and entertained there with all the pomp and protocol befitting royalty.

The first Audiencia, a royal court of appeal with jurisdiction throughout the Indies, was established in Santo Domingo. A bishop and members of several religious orders also took up residence there. A magnificent cathedral, begun in 1523, was completed in 1544. The first university in the New World was founded in Santo Domingo in 1538. The city's population in the mid sixteenth century was about 3500.[2]

In the countryside, Christopher Columbus had introduced a system of land and labor management know as the *repartimiento*. Under this system, settlers were granted large tracts of land in perpetuity, together with the labor of the Indians living on them. Finding that such a system left the authorities with too little control, the Crown in 1503 substituted a system known as the *encomienda*. The *encomienda* was the property of the Crown, and the Indians who lived on it were, in theory, under the Crown's protection. Spanish settlers were granted the use of the land and the services of its Indian tenants, but the grant might be revoked if the settlers were found to be abusing their tenants. In fact, abuse was scarcely abated, but the system served to strengthen the local authorities and centralize power, which had been dispersed by the *repartimiento*.

As the Indian population was rapidly declining, the importation of African slaves was begun in 1503. By 1520 the gold mines were almost exhausted; sugar was fast becoming the major export, and labor was provided almost entirely by black slaves.

The colony's decline began in the 1520s as the ambitious and adventurous pushed on to Mexico and Peru, where gold and silver were

2. Ian Bell, *The Dominican Republic* (Boulder, CO: Westview Press, 1981), p. 18.

being found in abundance. Santo Domingo remained an important way station, or staging area, for another 30 years, but the powers of its Audiencia were restricted as new courts were established in the more prosperous mainland colonies.

In 1564, the island's main inland cities, Santiago de los Caballeros and Concepción de la Vega, were destroyed by an earthquake. Meanwhile, English pirates had begun to prey on coastal settlements. In 1586 Sir Francis Drake laid siege to Santo Domingo, sacked and burned and left the city in ruins. The capital turned back an invasion staged by the British in 1655, but the Spanish authorities burned their own cities on Hispaniola's northern coast to prevent smuggling and to deny them to the French.

French settlements, several times destroyed by the Spaniards, continued to reappear. By the 1660s the French had de facto control of the western third of the island, but that control was not recognized by the Spanish Crown until the two countries signed the Treaty of Ryswick in 1697, ending a 12-year war. The French colony, known as Saint-Domingue, soon came to be one of the world's richest, while Spain's, on the remaining two-thirds of the island, languished.

Trading restrictions imposed by Spain on the colonies discouraged exports, except as contraband. Many sugar plantations in the south, subjected to raids by pirates, were abandoned. Absentee landlords showed little interest in their crops or their cattle. By 1730 the colony's population had dropped to 6000.

The economy began to recover, however, in 1740, with the opening of several ports to foreign commerce. New immigrants arrived, and by 1785 the colony had almost 150,000 inhabitants. About 40,000 of these were of Spanish descent, another 40,000 were black slaves, and the remainder were black or mulatto freedmen. The fact that freedmen constituted so large a proportion of the population and that the conditions of slavery had been less harsh in the Spanish colony meant that the slave revolt that was soon to come in Saint-Domingue did not strike so responsive a chord in Santo Domingo.[3]

Haitian Occupation (1822—1844)

Repercussions from the French Revolution in 1789 set off a confusing chain of events in Hispaniola. Racial tension had been mounting in

---

3. Rodman, *Quisqueya*, p. 23.

Saint-Domingue, and in 1791 Toussaint L'Ouverture led a slave revolt against the French planters and administrators. His black and mulatto rebels initially joined forces with the Spanish in Santo Domingo who were fighting the French colonists in the west. In 1794, however, learning that the new French government had abolished slavery in the colonies, L'Ouverture changed sides. He made common cause with the French forces to overwhelm the Spanish. When Spain ceded Santo Domingo to France in 1795, he became governor of the enlarged French colony.

The new order in what had been Santo Domingo, including the freeing of all slaves, horrified the Hispanic aristocracy, which migrated in large numbers to neighboring Spanish colonies. Napoleon Bonaparte, who soon rose to power in France, was not happy with L'Ouverture's rule either, and in 1802 he sent a military expedition to Santo Domingo. L'Ouverture was captured and sent back to France in irons, but black and mulatto forces in the western part of the island, now under the leadership of Jean Jacques Dessalines, defeated the French forces and declared independence for the historic area of Saint-Domingue, now renamed Haiti.

The French retained control of Santo Domingo until 1809, when the Spanish colonists, in league with the English, rebelled and won the colony back for Spain. But Spain showed little interest in its reconquered territory. Slavery had been reimposed, and some of the Hispanic elite that had taken refuge elsewhere returned. But agricultural production came to a standstill, and hunger was widespread. Conditions deteriorated until in 1821 the colonists rebelled again. This time it was the Spanish governor who was deported. The colonists declared their independence and sought union with the Republic of Gran Colombia, which had just been established by the South American Liberator, Simón Bolívar. But independence was not long to be savored, and Gran Colombia was not able to help. In 1822, encountering no resistance, Haitian president Jean-Pierre Boyer declared the entire island a single republic, under the flag and the laws of Haiti.

Thus began a period that for Dominicans lives on in infamy and paranoia. The former Spanish colony was subjected to rule by mulatto bureaucrats and black soldiers, speaking French and Creole and basing their legal system on the unfamiliar Napoleonic Code. The Church and many of the landowning families were deprived of their properties.

Haitian rule was not disadvantageous to all Dominicans, as slavery was again abolished, but commercial agriculture languished, and trade and shipping were paralyzed. Young men were drafted at the age of 16, and the university, lacking both students and teachers, closed down. The degradation of occupation was felt most intensely in Santo Domingo, and it was there that the movement to roll back the Haitians originated.

The nationalistic secret society, which came to be known as *La Trinitaria* (The Trinitarian), was organized in 1838 under the leadership of Juan Pablo Duarte, a young first-generation Dominican who had been educated in Europe. It was later joined by Ramón Mella and Francisco del Rosario Sánchez, who along with Duarte came to be considered national heroes. Within 5 years La Trinitaria had established a powerful network. It joined forces in 1843 with a Haitian movement to overthrow President Boyer and replace him with Charles Hérard. This was achieved, but Hérard, once in power, turned on the Dominican nationalists, many of whom were arrested or exiled. Nevertheless, the following year the nationalists succeeded in seizing the fortress in Santo Domingo. That day, February 27, 1844, was designated independence day for the new nation, now called the Dominican Republic.[4]

Uncertain Nationhood (1844–1916)

La Trinitaria, as personified by Duarte, Mella, and Sánchez, initially assumed control of the new state and sought to establish a democratic republic. But their rule was opposed by other armed groups that had sought to replace Haitian rule with protectorate status under some major power. One such group, led by General Pedro Santana, seized the capital in September 1844 and exiled the liberal leaders.

Santana was challenged, in turn, by another advocate of protectorate status, General Buenaventura Báez. The violent struggle between the two men was based on opportunism rather than ideology. They alternated in power, subjecting the country to turmoil, authoritarianism, and corruption until, in 1861, Santana arranged for Spain to reannex its former colony.

While Santana served as Captain General, Spanish officials once again replaced Dominicans in the military, in the bureaucracy, and in ecclesiastical posts. Spanish rule, this time, was extraordinarily inept.

4. Bell, *Dominican Republic*, pp. 27–29.

New taxes were imposed while the economy deteriorated, and corruption was blatant. Insurrection became increasingly effective, particularly in the Cibao region, and the Spanish forces, weakened by yellow fever, abandoned the island in 1865.

General Santana had died during the interlude of Spanish rule. The insurrectionists who took over from the fleeing Spaniards were soon squabbling among themselves, which enabled General Báez to seize power once again. There was little production or commerce left to tax in the Dominican Republic, so Báez, in an attempt to fill his government's empty coffers, tried to sell or lease Samaná Bay to the United States. Popular indignation at that move led to rebellion and to the overthrow of Báez in 1873. Báez's opponents, led by General Gregorio Luperon, formed the Blue party, which alternated in power with Báez's Red party until 1882.

More or less fair elections were held in 1882 for only the second time in the country's history, but the outcome proved to be disastrous. General Ulises Heureaux, who was elected president at that time, established a rigid dictatorship that was to last for 17 years.

Heureaux's rule differed little from that of its predecessors, except in its absolutism and its longevity. Heureaux relied on paranoic fear of Haiti, domestic terror, corruption, and foreign loans to maintain himself in power. He destroyed the incipient party system through a combination of cooptation and assassination. He distrusted and persecuted friends and supporters as well as enemies. He maintained a large network of spies at home and abroad, and ruthlessly crushed those who plotted against him or even gave evidence of independent thinking. Through it all, he maintained a facade of constitutional government and, in fact, used periodic elections effectively to keep opponents off balance. He increased the foreign debt tenfold, securing loans from European and U.S. financiers by mortgaging receipts from Dominican customs houses.

Heureaux's assassination in 1899 brought little relief. Iron-fisted dictatorship was followed by anarchy, as opponents of Heureaux contended for power, first with remnants of Heureaux's military establishment and later among themselves. Short-lived central governments lost control of the rural areas, as provincial bosses assembled their own armies. Even Ramón Cáceres, the assassin of Heureaux, who managed to rule—less harshly and more ably than most—from 1906 to 1911, was unable fully to subjugate rural bosses.

Meanwhile, by the turn of the century, the Dominican government had ceased to meet the interest payments on its foreign debt. European creditors began to threaten punitive action. The U.S. government, concerned about those threats and about the interests of U.S. creditors, particularly the San Domingo Improvement Company—and riding a wave of expansionist sentiment—stepped in and took over the collection of Dominican customs duties. Under an agreement signed reluctantly by Dominican president Carlos Morales in 1905, the United States returned 45 percent of the customs revenues to the Dominican government and distributed the other 55 percent among European and U.S. creditors. The agreement was replaced by a treaty, signed by the Cáceres government, 1907.

The assassination of Cáceres in 1911 plunged the country into chaos once again. Provisional and short-lived governments were unable to function within the terms of the customs agreement. With war looming in Europe, U.S. officials began to see political and strategic reasons, as well as economic ones, for controlling events in the Dominican Republic.

Occupation by the United States (1916–1924)

Already heavily involved in the making and unmaking of Dominican regimes and policies, the United States, in November 1915, presented to Dominican president Juan Isidro Jiménez a proposal that the United States assume full control of the republic's financial affairs and that the Dominican Army be replaced by a constabulary under U.S. command. When word of the proposal spread, Jiménez's position became untenable, and on May 1, 1916, he was impeached by the Dominican Congress. At that point, President Woodrow Wilson's secretary of state, Robert Lansing, asked Jiménez to request U.S. military aid. While Jiménez hesitated, U.S. Marines proceeded to disembark at the country's principal ports. Jiménez resigned on May 7, and General Desiderio Arias, in command of the Dominican Army, fled to the interior. Pursued by the marines, Arias surrendered in Santiago on July 6, 1916.

Unprepared for direct rule, the United States allowed the Dominican Congress to select a provisional president. But the one they selected, Dr. Francisco Henríquez y Carvajal, was unwilling to be a yes-man, and the United States withheld recognition. In November 1916 he resigned and left the country. The Congress was dissolved, and the United States was left with no alternative to direct martial law imposed by the occupation forces.

Beginning with the assumption of control over Cuba, Puerto Rico, and the Philippines at the conclusion of the Spanish American War (1898–1902), and following with the "liberation" of Panama from Colombia in 1903 and the occupation of Nicaragua in 1912 and Haiti in 1915, the United States had been more or less systematically expanding its sphere of influence and attempting to establish control, in particular, over Central America and much of the Caribbean. The invasion and occupation of the Dominican Republic—with fewer than 1 million inhabitants, 85 percent of whom were rural—was an episode of no great consequence in the sweep of U.S. history. For the Dominican Republic, of course, it was another matter; the consequences of U.S. occupation were enormous and enduring.

As in other countries under U.S. occupation at that time, the marines carried out a fairly extensive public works program. Road building was a major part of it, and one that, along with the modernization of communications, was viewed as essential for maintaining control. Altruistic motives and progressive notions were more readily apparent in the construction of schools and sanitation systems and in the expansion of education and public health programs. The boom in public works was not, however, an outright contribution from the United States. It was financed by U.S. private-sector investors rather than by the U.S. government; thus it swelled the already troublesome foreign debt.

The Wilson administration, distracted by World War I, had little attention to devote to the Dominican Republic. Thus the military government lacked a coherent and integrated set of policies. Apart from the trends already set in motion by U.S. occupation forces elsewhere and reinforced by the rotation of officials among the occupied areas, decisions tended to be made locally, on an ad hoc basis. While there was little direction from Washington, naval, marine, and State Department officials on the island were constantly subject to the influence of U.S. investors, traders, and planters with interests directly at stake.[5]

---

5. Bruce J. Calder, *The Impact of Intervention: The Dominican Republic during the U.S. Occupation of 1916–1924*. (Austin: University of Texas Press, 1984), p. 243.

Thus some of the many "reforms" undertaken were clearly beneficial to U.S. private interests. The tariff act of 1920, which reduced overall tariff rates by an average of 38 percent and placed some 250 items on the free-entry list, was a boon to U.S. merchants, who supplied more than 90 percent of the country's imports. The act was particularly offensive to Dominican leaders, as it meant a substantial loss of revenue for the republic, and the flood of new imports threatened the country's few existing industries. Even local food producers suffered as a result of the new competition.

Likewise, the land registration act of the same year served to expedite the expansion of the large, U.S.-owned sugar plantations. Following very closely a land registration plan that had been developed for the Philippines, it called, in particular, for the partition of communal land. Communal landholders and squatters without titles were displaced in large numbers as sugar companies and other commercial plantations added thousands upon thousands of acres to their properties. Even peasants who owned individual family plots were no match for corporations that could hire gaggles of lawyers.

The land tax, as introduced in 1919, taxed large landholdings at a higher rate than small ones. It might have been expected to benefit some large landholders at the expense of others, by forcing unproductive planters to sell to productive ones, but within a year the differential rate between large and small landholdings had been abolished, and by 1921 a well-organized tax boycott had virtually nullified the program.

In other areas, the consequences of U.S. occupation for the social system were mixed. The impact on Dominican culture was limited. The popularity of baseball grew with the presence of teams of U.S. Marines. In most areas, however, the culture of the occupying forces was scarcely seen as one to be emulated. In fact, defensive nationalism generated new interest and pride in things Dominican, such as folklore and the *merengue*, soon to become the national dance. Cutting nearer to the core of the social system, U.S. occupation forces inspired somewhat greater freedom for women, but at the same time introduced greater rigidity into what had been a relatively flexible pattern of race relations.

Among the highest priorities of the U.S. occupation forces in the Dominican Republic, as elsewhere, had been the creation of a constabulary force. The force was to replace all other armed bodies—in the Dominican case, the army, the navy, the frontier guard, and the

Guardia Republicana. It was assumed that there was no function or justification for the maintenance of a military establishment, that no external threat existed, and that, should one materialize, it would be dealt with by the United States. Thus the function of the constabulary, under U.S. guidance, was to be that of policing the nation and keeping a lid on rural and urban unrest. The constabulary was to avoid alignment with any local political faction; its primary base of support was to be the U.S. military.

The new force, created by executive order of the U.S. military government in April 1917, was called the *Guardia Nacional Dominicana*, or Dominican National Guard. By 1918 the full complement of 1200 men had been recruited. The nucleus of the new Guard came from the now defunct Guardia Republicana, an unruly group, notorious for preying on civilians.

All ranks above lieutenant were reserved for North Americans. In fact, few Dominicans having the required education and status wanted the stigma of serving the occupation forces, so temporary commissions were given to enlisted men among the U.S. Marines. Dominicans recruited to serve under them generally came from the lower middle class. One such recruit was Rafael Trujillo, who joined the Guard in 1919.

One of the most important responsibilities of the Guard was to supplement the efforts of U.S. Marines in putting down a guerrilla uprising in the east. The seeds of insurgency, particularly in the provinces of Seybo and San Pedro de Macorís, antedated the occupation; in those areas the expansion of modern sugar-producing plantations was already displacing peasants who had engaged in subsistence farming, leaving them landless and desperate. Marines were detached virtually on disembarkation to protect a U.S.-owned sugar estate, Consuelo, north of the city of San Pedro de Macorís.[6]

But the occupation itself contributed to the spread of insurgency, as the land registration act and other measures adopted by the military government accelerated the displacement of subsistence farmers. Furthermore, tactics employed by the marines and their Dominican understudies and informants, including the brutalization of entire communities in areas that had been "cordoned off," alienated the population and intensified nationalistic fervor.

Insurgency in the Dominican Republic was by no means an isolated phenomenon. Guerrillas—who, in those days, the United States called

---

6. *Ibid.*, p. 134.

bandits—had materialized in virtually all the countries under U.S. occupation. Though no leaders emerged in the Dominican Republic of the stature of Nicaragua's Sandino, the Dominican insurgents held out against the superior arms of the U.S. occupation forces for 5 years. The insurgency ended, with hundreds imprisoned and hundreds more accepting amnesty, only after the United States had drawn up plans for withdrawal.

A factor leading more directly to the U.S. withdrawal was the mounting resistance of articulate, urban Dominicans. Owing perhaps to the indifference of urban upper and middle classes to the plight of peasants, and perhaps also to censorship, there was little notable urban support for the guerrilla campaign in the east. Nevertheless, by 1920 specific abuses associated with martial law, together with the humiliation of foreign occupation, had spurred urban Dominicans to the organization of a more effective nationalist movement. Under the banner of the Unión Nacional Dominicana, nationalists increased their agitation and acts of defiance at home, while mounting an international campaign of diplomacy and propaganda against the occupation.

The international campaign caused embarrassment to the Wilson administration, which began in late 1920 to draw up plans for withdrawal. The U.S. government soon found, however, that it is far easier to launch an intervention than to withdraw from one. The U.S. occupation forces were determined, for example, to ensure that those who most actively resisted their presence not profit from their departure. In that they were successful; when the United States finally withdrew in 1924, it was not the Dominican nationalists but the U.S.-sponsored constabulary, under the leadership of Rafael Trujillo, that moved in to fill the power vacuum.

The Era of Trujillo

The U.S. Marines, before departing, had overseen the election of the aging General Horacio Vásquez to the presidency. Vásquez, however, enjoyed little support, and when, in 1930, he attempted to extend his term, he was overthrown by the followers of Rafael Estrella Ureña. Estrella Ureña had been assisted in this move by Trujillo, commander of the constabulary, now called the National Army. Once Vásquez had been deposed, however, Trujillo refused to allow Estrella Ureña to take office. Instead, after intimidating the opposition through a series of murders, Trujillo had himself elected president. He "won," in fact, with more votes than there were eligible voters.[7]

As a sugar plantation guard, and later as an officer climbing up the ranks of the constabulary during the years of U.S. occupation, Trujillo had learned the arts and the arguments of counterinsurgency. From the marines he learned the techniques of intelligence, and after their departure he organized an intelligence service to spy, initially on behalf of Vásquez, on meetings and other political events. He also learned the importance and the means of maintaining U.S. support. With this background, with such attributes as limitless greed and ruthlessness, and with the well-bought loyalty of the now well-trained and well-armed constabulary, Trujillo established, over a 30-year period, a dictatorship that was as nearly totalitarian as the country's level of economic and technological development would accommodate. By the late 1950s, the generalissimo had at least seven categories of intelligence agencies, all spying on each other as well as on the public. All citizens were obliged to carry both identification cards and good-conduct passes from the secret police.

Trujillo passed up no opportunity to enhance either his power or his wealth. A devastating hurricane that swept through Santo Domingo during his first year in office provided his rationale for ruling by decree. It also provided relief funds to pilfer and development funds to pocket in the process of rebuilding. When opponents of his regime were imprisoned or victimized by "accidents," their properties were confiscated by the state, which meant that they came into the possession of the Trujillo family.

Though he relished humiliating the aristocracy, Trujillo was able to secure their acquiescence through a combination of carrots and sticks. Any hint of disloyalty was likely to result in selective taxation, whereas cooperation with the regime entitled one to some portion of the spoils.

The Partido Dominicano (PD), which Trujillo founded in 1931, was the only party allowed to function until 1947, when his "democratization" propaganda campaign called for a show of opposition. The party was funded, in part, by automatic 10 percent deductions from the salaries of all government employees.

The republic remained under U.S. financial tutelage until 1940. That meant, among other things, a lid on the public debt, a continuation of

---

7. Howard J. Wiarda and Michael J. Kryzanek, *The Dominican Republic: A Caribbean Crucible* (Boulder, CO: Westview Press, 1982), p. 35.

the very lenient tariff policy, and, after 1934, a reinstatement of the customs receivership. Recovery from the depression years was slow, and Trujillo called for sacrifice—nothing new, of course, to the country's working classes. World War II, however, brought increased demands for Dominican exports, and an era of increased prosperity—especially for Trujillo and his friends and relatives—was under way.

In general, the 1940s and early 1950s witnessed economic growth and another boom in public works. It was hardly coincidental that new roads often led to Trujillo's plantations and factories, and new harbors benefited Trujillo's shipping and export enterprises. Ultimately, Trujillo, along with his relatives and friends, owned well over half of the country's economic assets. They employed almost half of the labor force directly, and another 35 percent were employed by the government. By the time of his death, Trujillo was reckoned to be one of the two or three richest men in the world with a fortune estimated at from several hundred million to a billion dollars.

Trujillo's savagery became apparent in 1937 when government troops, on his orders, massacred some 20,000 to 25,000 Haitian illegal immigrants, especially squatters in the border provinces. That episode brought him some bad press in the United States and elsewhere, but with the onrush of World War II it was soon forgotten. In years to come, many thousands of Trujillo's political opponents were to be imprisoned, tortured, and murdered; but only when his dirty work reached beyond Dominican shores—as in the 1956 kidnapping of Spaniard Jesús María de Galíndez in New York, and his subsequent murder—did the external world express much concern.

The Catholic Church was generally supportive, or at least acquiescent, until 1960. Police brutality in retaliating against a revolutionary plot aborted the previous year was openly condemned by the new papal nuncio and the bishops. Trujillo began then to persecute individual clergymen. Eventually he tried to devise ways of killing the pope, and on the night Trujillo was assassinated he had issued an order for the arrest of all bishops.[8]

In his relations with the United States, Trujillo left little to chance. His economic concessions were generous, and no ideological commitment stood in the way of behavior becoming an ally. Despite sympathies with the fascist cause, he responded to the attack on Pearl Harbor by declaring war on the Axis. When the cold war came into vogue, he

---

8. Bell, *Dominican Republic*, p. 74.

declared himself the hemisphere's foremost anticommunist. In the same spirit, his domestic enemies were labeled communists. He cultivated a benign image in the United States by hiring U.S. public relations firms and lobbyists and making generous campaign contributions to members of the U.S. Congress. He also sweetened the alliance by offering lucrative business deals to U.S. businessmen and politicians.

By 1960, however, Trujillo was becoming an embarrassment to his erstwhile U.S. benefactors. Dictatorship, in general, had fallen into disrepute, and one after another of Latin America's tyrants had been toppled by popular movements. Even the hemisphere's other remaining tyrants, such as Nicaragua's Somoza and Paraguay's Stroessner, made a point of keeping their distance from Trujillo.

Trujillo became convinced that an abortive plot against him in 1959 had been supported by Venezuela's newly elected civilian president, Rómulo Bétancourt. He retaliated by having one of his thugs attempt to assassinate Bétancourt.[9] Bétancourt, in turn, brought the matter before the Organization of American States (OAS) in 1960, where Trujillo was censured. Member states voted unanimously to sever diplomatic relations and impose economic sanctions.

Meanwhile, the United States had been attempting to bring action against Cuba's new revolutionary regime in the OAS, but kept finding that Latin American's democratic governments preferred to talk about Trujillo. Moreover, it had come to be feared that Trujillo, far from being a bastion against communism, might unite the country against him and bring on a successful revolution. In February of 1960 President Dwight Eisenhower asked the National Security Council's Special Group on Central Intelligence Agency (CIA) covert operations to consider aiding Trujillo's enemies.[10]

On May 3, 1961, Trujillo, nearing 70 years of age, was being driven to visit his mistress when his car was ambushed and he was shot to death. His assassins were Dominicans, business and military leaders. The guns had been supplied by the CIA.

---

9. It is not clear whether Trujillo knew of Bétancourt's involvement or only suspected it, but Social Christian leader Alfonso Moreno Martínez, who was in exile in Venezuela at the time and was a party to the plot, says that it ws indeed backed by Bétancourt (Moreno Martínez, interviews with the author, Santo Domingo, November 28–29, 1982, and January 2 and 12, 1985).
10. Bernard Diederich, *Trujillo: The Death of the Goat* (Boston: Little, Brown, 1978), p. 40.

3
CONTEMPORARY HISTORY

A Botched Palace Coup

The assassination of Trujillo was to have been merely the first step toward a complete change of government. But several of the conspirators' plans were botched. The general who was to have announced on the radio Trujillo's death and the change of government got cold feet and disappeared. Meanwhile, Trujillo's driver, who had been only slightly wounded, hitched a ride back to the capital and reported to Trujillo's followers. Trujillo's eldest son, Ramfis, returned immediately from Paris to take charge of the investigation and retribution. Within a few days, all but three of the more than two dozen conspirators had been rounded up. Ultimately all were killed—several of them slowly, by torture. Two of the three who escaped were Antonio Imbert Barrera and Luis Amiama Tío, who, with CIA help, had masterminded the conspiracy.

Joaquín Balaguer, formerly Trujillo's presidential secretary, was serving as titular president at the time of Trujillo's death, but Ramfis, supported by the armed forces, remained in command. The strength of that command was soon countered, however, by pressures from the United States and the OAS for liberalization. Public opinion, so long suppressed, was also begining to make itself felt. Ramfis and Balaguer bowed tentatively to these pressures. Exiles were allowed to return, and political parties began to form. Strikes and demonstrations took place.

It became clear that there was to be·no international recognition for the government and no resolution to the political standoff as long as Trujillo's heirs remained in the country. After fierce rioting in October,

Ramfis sent his "wicked uncles," the generalissimo's brothers Héctor and Arismendi, out of the country. But they returned in November with murder on their minds—plotting a takeover and a "final solution" for the enemies of Trujillismo. Their plot was frustrated by the swift action of Air Force Commander Pedro Rodríguez Echavarría, who was surprised, in turn, by the appearance of a U.S. naval flotilla just off the coast. During the third week of November, Ramfis and the "wicked uncles" departed for the last time, taking with them a considerable portion of the republic's movable wealth.

Dominicans, believing at last that they were rid of Trujillismo, began to celebrate in earnest. Everything bearing the face or the name of Trujillo was trashed. The capital, which had been renamed Ciudad Trujillo, reverted to its original name. All Trujillo property was confiscated by the state. And suddenly there were no Trujillo loyalists to be found.

General Echavarría now became the power behind Balaguer's titular presidency. In December Balaguer succumbed to U.S. and local pressures to draw members of the newly formed conservative opposition, the National Civic Union (UCN) into a Council of State. The two surviving assassins of Trujillo, Imbert and Amiama, now enjoying amnesty and commissioned as generals, were also appointed to the seven-member council. The council was to serve as a legislature and to share executive responsibility. The opposition, however, remained restive.

In January 1962 the UCN publicly called for a popular uprising against the government. General Echavarría responded by detaining the members of the new Council of State. This coup was aborted within 48 hours, as a general strike brought the capital to a standstill, and U.S. officials pointed out to other Dominican military officers how much the country stood to lose in aid and trade. Army officers arrested Echavarría and his closest air force associates and shipped them, along with Balaguer, who had taken asylum with the papal nuncio, to exile in Puerto Rico.[1]

The liberated council now assumed titular executive authority until it could be replaced by a duly elected president. Elections were sched-

---

1. Marino Vinicio ("Vincho") Castillo, Balaguer's friend and, at that time, his minister of labor, says that Balaguer had planned several months earlier to resign in January and that the oligarchy forced him out, rather than allow him to resign, in order to damage his prospects for winning elective office in the future. (Vincho Castillo, interview with the author, Santo Domingo, January 4, 1985).

uled for December 20. The race soon narrowed to a two-way one between Viriato Fiallo, a physician and leader of the UCN, and Juan Bosch, a social scientist and leader of the Dominican Revolutionary party (PRD). The UCN, established by business and professional leaders with little program other than ridding the country of Trujillismo, attracted other elements of the upper classes, as well as the Church hierarchy, and came to be seen as representing the conservative alternative. The PRD, founded by Bosch in 1939 while he was in exile in Puerto Rico, was self-consciously a party of the democratic left. It appealed to students and middle-class intellectuals, but its support came overwhelmingly from peasants and the urban working classes.

In his campaign rhetoric, Bosch trumped his opponent by running, not against Trujillismo, but against the oligarchy. His approach was to treat the Trujillo era as a ghost of the past—to erase it, rather than to keep the issue alive by seeking vengeance against collaborators. Thus, in addition to his ideologically compatible constituency, he attracted support from a large contingent of strange bedfellows.[2]

More than 90 percent of the republic's eligible voters turned out for the election. Bosch won by a landslide, capturing about 64 percent of the vote to 32 percent for Fiallo. The PRD also won more than two-thirds of the seats in each of the two houses of Congress.

A Short-Lived Democracy

Bosch was sworn in as president of the republic on February 27, 1963. He clearly attempted to be true to his campaign promises and responsive to his political base. The new constitution promulgated by his government in April was modern, secular, and liberal. It offered new protections and advantages to peasants and urban laborers. It separated Church and state and legalized divorce. It sought to establish civilian dominance over the military, and it guaranteed full respect for civil liberties. Thus it antagonized all of the most powerful elements of the traditional privileged minority: landowners, businessmen, the Church, and the military.

The landowning class was disturbed when Bosch began to distribute land to the peasants, even though it was land that had been confiscated from Trujillo. Freedom of expression and assemblage also proved

2. Castillo, interview.

unnerving to elements in the military and police forces, who had spent their careers suppressing such freedoms, and to whom all reformists sounded like "communists."[3] Bosch also made a point of seeking aid and investment from European countries as a means of establishing economic independence and counterbalancing U.S. influence. Not surprisingly, some U.S. officials saw this as an affront.

It would be unrealistic and misleading to speak of *the* U.S. attitude toward the Bosch government, or even of *the* attitude of the Kennedy administration. As has often been the case, especially when a liberal occupied the Oval Office, there were many attitudes and many conflicting agendas. Not only did the attitudes of U.S. business tycoons, who never lack access or influence, differ from those of John F. Kennedy's more liberal supporters, but there were important differences of opinion and approach among U.S. Democratic party liberals with regard to the Bosch government. Finally, according to several accounts from politically diverse quarters, while the president himself supported Bosch's government wholeheartedly (it was, after all, exemplary of the thrust of his newly launched Alliance for Progress), Kennedy's aims were sabotaged by his own foreign affairs bureaucracy.

In exile during the Trujillo years, Bosch had come into close association with the so-called Caribbean Legion, a group of political leaders of Central American and Caribbean states—some in power but most in exile—who conspired against the region's tyrannies. The legion and its offspring, the Institute for Political Education, established in Costa Rica, were supported by U.S. liberals and, for a time at least, by the U.S. government, with funds channeled through the CIA. Its leaders included Bétancourt of Venezuela, José ("Pepe") Figueres of Costa Rica, and Luis Múñoz Marín of Puerto Rico.

One of Bosch's closest advisers and confidents in Costa Rica was Sacha Volman, an émigré from Bessarabia, who had close ties with U.S. socialists and social democrats of the Americans for Democratic Action (ADA) and, after Kennedy assumed the presidency, with the White House. Volman went to the Dominican Republic in 1961, ahead

---

3. Bosch once surprised his supporters and political allies by announcing that he would prohibit a demonstration by teachers demanding higher pay. When Alfonso Moreno Martínez, leader of the PRSC, interceded in behalf of the teachers, Bosch told him that he was afraid to allow the teachers to march because, with the slightest provocation, the military and police would shoot them all. On Moreno's suggestion a compromise was arranged whereby the teachers could march, but only where the police agreed to permit it (Moreno Martínez, interview with the author).

of Bosch, to begin building a base for the PRD. In particular, he helped to organize the Federation of Peasant Brotherhoods (FENHERCA), and later he established in Santo Domingo the semiofficial Inter-American Center for Social Studies (CIDES).[4]

Volman maintains that he was never a CIA officer, as such. The agency's Western Hemisphere division had been colonized by former officers of J. Edgar Hoover's Federal Bureau of Investigation (FBI), for whom Volman had the utmost contempt. But, reporting directly to the White House, Volman had access to CIA funds, which he says he used at cross-purposes to those of the Western Hemisphere division. Volman also says that Bosch requested—and was given—the CIA station chief of his choice. The officer was transferred from Bolivia at Bosch's bidding.

By contrast, the Kennedy administration's ambassador to Santo Domingo, John Bartlow Martin, was not predisposed to sympathy with Bosch and the PRD. Covering the republic earlier, as a journalist, Martin had called the PRD a "bunch of thugs." Martin had not been a member of the Kennedy camp but rather had been appointed at the behest of Adlai Stevenson, in payment of a political debt. Like Volman, Martin spent a great deal of time with Bosch and advised him on many matters, but Martin was also personally friendly with members of the Dominican oligarchy.[5]

Fearing nationalization, among other things, U.S. businessmen had always been uneasy about Bosch. The U.S. military and police advisers were unhappy because Bosch was unenthusiastic about counterinsurgency and riot-control training. While the Council of State had ruled, the National Police, under U.S. tutelage, had been increased in size from 3000 to 10,000 men. But Bosch discontinued the U.S. police-training program.

Moreover, some U.S. officials, like Dominican conservatives, were disturbed that the freedom of expression tolerated by the Bosch government extended even to Marxists. Even though local communist groups were very small and weak,[6] Ambassador Martin, among others, feared that such exposure for Marxist ideas, coupled with what he saw as Bosch's administrative incompetence, might create conditions that would enable the communists to take over.

4. Sacha Volman, interview with the author, Santo Domingo, January 14, 1985.
5. Volman, interview.
6. Only 2 years earlier, those same supposedly fearsome communist groups had been working with the CIA to undermine Trujillo.

Throughout the summer of 1963, anticommunist demonstrations were staged around the country by Bosch's right-wing opponents. Ironically in view of its CIA connection, the bête noir of the anticommunist activists was the research and planning institution, CIDES, under the direction of Sacha Volman. Rumors had been spread that CIDES was planning a communist takeover.

The Bosch government lasted only 7 months. On September 25, while Bosch and his cabinet were in session in the National Palace, troops surrounded the palace. They proceeded to seize Bosch and his civilian cabinet members. The minister of the armed forces, Major General Viñas Román, who had been meeting with them, was not seized; he was a party to the conspiracy, as were all the chiefs of staff. Bosch, and later his vice-president, were bundled off to Puerto Rico. Other cabinet members were subsequently released, but the National Assembly was dissolved.

The agitation of Bosch's enemies in business and politics, instigated in particular by the oligarchy, served to create a climate propitious for a coup d'état; the coup itself was spearheaded by Air Force Colonel Elías Wessín y Wessín, a virulent anticommunist, and his colleagues from the Armed Forces Education Center (CEFA) at the San Isidro Air Force Base. Others prominently involved in the conspiracy, apart from the armed forces ministers and the chiefs of staff, included the chief of the National Police and the surviving assassins of Trujillo, Generals Imbert and Amiama Tío.

There were, even then, a coterie of military officers who were loyal to the PRD and to Bosch, but they made no move at that time to save his government. In defending his inaction, Colonel Francisco Caamaño Deñó later said that there had been no way for Bosch's military loyalists to protect his government because although Bosch was aware of the conspiracy against him, he was not willing to authorize any countermeasures.[7] Balaguer—no friend, at that time, of the oligarchy—reportedly tried to use his influence with the military to head off the overthrow of Bosch, but to no avail.[8]

The stance of the United States with respect to the overthrow of Bosch has long been shrouded in mystery, perhaps because of the divisions within the inner circles of the Kennedy administration, not to

---

7. First Lieutenant Claudio Caamaño, interview with the author, Santo Domingo, January 15, 1985.
8. Castillo, interview.

mention the obvious divisions within and among the various U.S. agencies. The National Confederation of Free Laborers (CONATRAL), organized and sustained by the American Institute for Free Labor Development (AIFLD)—a strange bedfellow arrangement of the AFL−CIO, AID, and CIA—had been prominently involved in the anti-Bosch agitation preceding the coup. Ambassador Martin maintains that he sought to head off the coup after he got wind of it, but was unable to reach U.S. military advisers by telephone. Bosch himself reportedly cried on hearing of Kennedy's assassination,[9] but he later charged the United States with conspiracy in the overthrow of his government.

Volman has stated that Ambassador Martin had plenty of advance notice about the coup, but failed to take action. Thereupon Volman, bypassing the embassy, placed a call to Kennedy's advisers in the White House. Kennedy, in turn, contacted Bosch and asked what he might do to prevent the coup. Kennedy even offered to send in U.S. troops, but Bosch declined.[10]

Meanwhile, U.S. military attaché Colonel Fritz Long, along with his colleague, a Colonel Cash, had reportedly been conspiring with representatives of the oligarchy and the militantly anticommunist CEFA group to topple the Bosch government. While the roles of Colonels Long and Cash appear to be common knowledge among Dominican political leaders, it is not known whether they were acting on their own or on orders from superiors in the Pentagon.[11]

Subsequently, Kennedy sent one of his own confidants in the U.S. military, a Colonel Reed, to the Dominican Republic to investigate the prospects for a countercoup that would return Bosch to power. Reed reportedly spoke, in turn, with former leaders of the Senate and the Chamber of Deputies, asking each if he would be willing to head an interim government, anticipating the return of Bosch. Each said he would be pleased to head a new government, but not to relinquish it to Bosch.[12]

Upon the overthrow of Bosch, Kennedy had promptly withdrawn the U.S. ambassador and suspended economic aid. He never recognized the government of the "Triumvirate" set up by the victorious

9. Castillo, interview.
10. Volman, interview.
11. The roles of Long and Cash were mentioned to me by several persons involved in Dominican politics at the time, including Volman, Castillo, and Moreno Martínez.
12. Castillo, interview.

conspirators, but 2 months after the coup, Kennedy himself was assassinated. Within less than a month of assuming the U.S. presidency, Lyndon Johnson renewed diplomatic relations with the Dominican government and restored economic aid.

An Abortive Revolution

To replace the elected government, the Dominican military established a three-man civilian junta that was to serve under military tutelage. The Bosch government's constitution was nullified, along with much of the PRD-sponsored legislation and the most important of the European line-of-credit arrangements. In October the dissolved Congress met secretly and declared the former president of the Chamber of Deputies, José Rafael Molina Ureña, constitutional president of the republic; he was soon arrested and sent to join Bosch in Puerto Rico.

In December the armed forces tracked down an amalgam of communist guerrillas and pro-Bosch college students, carrying the banner of the proscribed Fourteenth of June movement, in the Cordillera Central. Sixteen of them, including the movement's leader, Manuel Tavares Justo, were killed—after they had surrendered to government forces—and the rest were taken prisoner. Emilio de los Santos, a jurist who had been serving as leader of the governing junta, now known as the Triumvirate, resigned in protest over the massacre; he was replaced by a businessman, Donald Reid Cabral.

Apparently seeking to conciliate opinion in the United States, the Trumvirate promised to schedule elections. The elections were not in fact to take place, but U.S. aid began to flow freely. There was never much to show for it, however, as corruption assumed impressive dimensions.

Plotting against the Triumvirate was continuous and multifactional. One of the early plots to displace the Triumvirate involved Balaguer (still in exile) and his close associate Marino Vinicio ("Vincho") Castillo, along with Colonel Pedro Santiago Rodríguez Echavarría, younger brother of the general who had staged an abortive coup in early 1962. Most of the plotters were arrested. Castillo went into hiding in Boca Chica.[13]

13. Castillo, interview.

Other disaffected military and party leaders had begun to meet in late 1963 to plot the demise of the Triumvirate. The military conspirators divided loosely into three factions or tendencies. One favored the reinstatement of Bosch, another, a short-term junta to take certain measures and call new elections, and a third indefinite military rule.[14]

Reid Cabral, a prominent member of the oligarchy, never had any significant popular following, and resentment against him increased after he imposed economic austerity measures in an attempt to cope with the mounting foreign debt. Finally, in early 1965, he attempted to gain control over the armed forces, dismissing the secretary of state for the armed forces, General Viñas Román, and assuming that post for himself. This brought about temporary unity among the several military factions that had been plotting, each with its own purposes, the overthrow of the Triumvirate.

Once the Triumvirate was deposed, on April 24, the right-wing plotters, led by General Wessín y Wessín, were quickly overwhelmed by other plotters, mainly young army colonels associated with the PRD underground opposition. Civilians in the PRD also swung into action, as José Francisco Peña Gómez, a young lawyer who was leading the party in the absence of Bosch, announced on the radio in Santo Domingo that the movement to restore the constitutional government was under way. Thousands of unarmed people took to the streets as the pro-Bosch, or Constitutionalist, troops occupied the presidential palace. Molina Ureña, already back from exile, was sworn into service as interim president until Bosch could return.

In alliance at that time with the Dominican Revolutionary party, the Social Christian Revolutionary party (PRSC), a party of center–left Christian Democrats, endorsed the Constitu onalist movement, as did the Fourteenth of June movement and two small Communist parties, the Dominican Communist party (PCD) and the Dominican Popular Movement (MPD).

Initially, the anti-Bosch military officers, with the exception of General Wessín y Wessín, showed no inclination to challenge the Constitutionalists in battle, but by late afternoon on April 25, they had been persuaded by Wessín y Wessín and, more important, by agents of the U.S. government, to form a junta and take up

---

14. Caamaño, interview.

arms.[15] This group became known as the Loyalists. On April 26, its air force contingent bombarded the National Palace and other strongholds of the Constitutionalists. At the Duarte Bridge, the major point of entry into the city from the east, scarcely armed civilians suffered heavy casualties as they repeatedly repelled the tanks of the Loyalists. Colonel Francisco Caamaño Deñó, a U.S.-trained officer, named interior minister by interim president Molina Ureña, emerged at that time as both an able military leader and a charismatic figure. Along with Navy Captain Manuel Montes Arache, he rallied the military supporters of the PRD cause. By April 27 the Constitutionalists were in control of Santo Domingo and appeared to be about to take Santiago.

The first contingent of U.S. Marines arrived on April 28. It was announced at that time that President Johnson had authorized the intervention in order to protect American lives; in fact, the intent was to suppress the Constitutionalists. By April 30, when the matter was brought to the attention of the Organization of American States, some 23,000 U.S. troops had taken up positions in Santo Domingo and throughout the country.[16]

On May 2, President Johnson announced that "what began as a popular democratic revolution, . . . very shortly moved and was taken over and really seized and placed into the hands of a band of communist conspirators." This was alleged to have happened on April 27, when, as a consequence of Bosch's inability or unwillingness to return from Puerto Rico to the Dominican Republic, the leadership of the rebel force passed from Colonel Miguel Angel Ramírez to Colonel Francisco Caamaño Deñó. John Bartlow Martin, now President Johnson's special envoy, had attributed to Caamaño the capability of becoming "his country's Castro." Later the names of 58 communists allegedly involved in the fighting were released by U.S. officials to substantiate the claim. The list had been drawn up hastily. Enterprising U.S. journalists found that some of the persons named were dead,

---

15. First Lieutenant Claudio Caamaño says that his uncle, Colonel Francisco Caamaño Deñó, received an intimidating call from the U.S. military attaché on April 25. According to Claudio, who answered the telephone and stayed on the line, Colonel Caamaño told him, in effect, to mind his own business, and hung up on him.
16. Volman says that he had tried to call the White House to plead against invasion but that Johnson's advisers would not take his call. Failing in that attempt, he placed a call to Adlai Stevenson, who had been retained by Johnson as U.S. ambassador to the United Nations. Stevenson responded, however, that the United States could not tolerate violence, and he declined to intercede.

some were in prison or out of the country, and some clearly were not communists.[17]

The OAS council, on April 30, had called for an immediate cease-fire between forces favoring restoration of the Bosch government and the opposing military junta. The Tenth Meeting of Consultation of Foreign Ministers, which convened on May 1 and met throughout 1965 and early 1966, dispatched a five-nation peace commission. On May 6, the delegate of the "loyalist" military junta, who had been seated at the insistence of the United States, provided the vote required for OAS adoption of the U.S.-sponsored resolution creating the Inter-American Peace Force (IAPF). Chile, Ecuador, Mexico, Peru, and Uruguay voted against it; Venezuela abstained. Charged with maintaining peace and restoring constitutional government, the IAPF absorbed the U.S. forces already operating in the country and became a multilateral cover for the pursuit of U.S. military goals. Under nominal Brazilian command, but in fact under U.S. command, the peace force was composed mainly of U.S. troops, with token contingents from Brazil, Paraguay, Honduras, Costa Rica, and Nicaragua. After a bloody fight in mid June, resulting in several thousand deaths, both Dominican factions, each for its own reasons, called for the withdrawal of the peace force; it nevertheless continued to function through the spring of 1966.

In June 1965 the OAS created a three-man Ad Hoc Committee to act as its mediator between the warring factions, but by late summer the Constitutionalist rebellion had been subdued. A peace agreement between Loyalists and Constitutionalists was signed on August 31. Under the agreement, or "Institutional Act," leaders of both military factions were to be sent abroad—in effect, exiled—to diplomatic posts. The Ad Hoc Committee conducted negotiations resulting in the installation of Provisional President Héctor García Godoy, a member of the Santiago oligarchy who had served as Bosch's foreign minister, on September 3. He was to serve for 10 months, presiding, under the supervision of the IAPF, over the elections of June 1, 1966.

A Suspect Election

All major parties held national conventions. Campaigning, which had begun the previous fall, officially opened on March 1, 1966. The

17. Jerome Slater, *Intervention and Negotiation: The United States and the Dominican Republic* (New York: Harper & Row, 1970), pp. 35–39.

general uncertainty and continued threats and incidents of violence were political issues. So, too, were electoral procedures, voter qualifications, and official recognition of parties.

The only functioning party ever to win a national election, the Dominican Revolutionary party, again nominated Juan Bosch for president. Bosch had finally returned to Santo Domingo at the end of September 1965. Again the PRD platform called for revolutionary social and economic change within a framework of political democracy, and again the party sought support among intellectuals and among the urban and rural lower classes who had previously elected him. PRD candidates condemned the intervention by the United States and the OAS, criticized the provisional government, and praised the Constitutionalist movement. They also stressed the fact that Balaguer was favored by the United States.

The Social Christian Revolutionary party, founded in exile in mid 1961 by young Christian socialists, supported Bosch's candidacy in accordance with an agreement of February 1965, in which it had joined the Dominican Revolutionary party in pledging to restore his administration. Its leadership tended to be antimilitary, antioligarchy, and ambivalent toward the United States. The party was already plagued, however, by factionalism.

The Reformist party (Partido Reformista—PR) had been founded in July 1963 by Balaguer, who was at that time in exile in New York. It was legally recognized by the Triumvirate government in April 1964. After Balaguer's return to the country on June 28, 1965, it became his vehicle for seeking the presidency. Its platform in that campaign did not differ greatly from that of the PRD, although emphasis was on order and stability rather than on reform. It concentrated on winning business support, the female vote (presumed to be heavily influenced by the Catholic Church), and the relatively conservative rural vote. Heading a coalition that hoped to hold the balance of power in the event that neither Bosch nor Balaguer won a clear majority was Rafael F. Bonnelly, who had presided over the 1962 Council of State.

Balaguer won the election on July 1, 1966, by a landslide, with 57 percent of the vote to 39 percent for Bosch. His Reformist party also won a substantial majority in both houses.

In retrospect, it seems remarkable that at the time the U.S. media and, in general, U.S. public opinion accepted the election and its outcome as legitimate. After all, Bosch and the PRD had swept the elections just 4 years earlier, and a year earlier had been on the verge of winning again in the streets the victory of the polling booth that had been seized from them through a military coup. The elections of 1966 took place while the country was under military occupation by U.S. Marines, an occupation that had come about precisely to prevent a victory by the Constitutionalists and the reinstatement of Bosch in the presidency. A former CIA officer, Ray Cline, has recounted a meeting with President Johnson in which he described Balaguer and recommended him for the Dominican presidency. Johnson's response, he says, was, "Get this guy in office down there!"[18]

The Johnson administration sent a team of observers, some of whom were sympathetic to Bosch, to Santo Domingo for the election. Most of them conceded that they saw no evidence of coercion at the polling places, but that is hardly surprising, as they were able to visit only a very small proportion of such polling places and were escorted by official military forces. Moreover, they had no way of evaluating the procedures involved in collecting ballot boxes and in counting the votes, procedures that were likewise supervised by military and police forces. In fact, there were reports, generally overlooked by the major media in the United States, of irregularities at the polls: of voters being transported from one place to another, of widespread forgery of identification cards, and of commandeering and switching of ballot boxes. It was also reported that soldiers and policemen staged an impressive show of force in every sizable town on election day and that some PRD supporters spoke of feeling intimidated.[19]

The overall total of votes cast in 1966 was 25 percent higher than the total for 1962, and 87 percent higher in Santo Domingo, where Bosch's 80 percent margin in 1962 was shaved to 63 percent. Balaguer's margin of victory corresponded almost exactly to the increase in the overall vote, as officially reported.

It is quite possible, of course, that, with or without fraud, Balaguer would have won the election.[20] To many Dominicans, Balaguer's candidacy seemed to promise a new era of tranquillity, while Bosch's

---

18. Edward S. Herman and Frank Brodhead, *Demonstration Elections: U.S.-Staged Elections in the Dominican Republic, Vietnam and El Salvador* (Boston: South End Press, 1984), p. 46.
19. Ibid., pp. 40–42.
20. Balaguer has since proven his electoral appeal. It was at that time, however, untested. His old friend and collaborator, Vincho Castillo, says that given the circumstances of the elections of 1966 and of the 1970s, it was not until Balaguer almost won the presidential election of 1980 that he was able to prove his popularity.

augured a continuation of civil strife. Furthermore, it is clear that with much of the peasantry Balaguer was genuinely popular. It is scarcely credible, however, that there were circumstances under which the U.S. and IAPF occupation forces and their Dominican allies would have allowed Bosch and the PRD to win. In the course of defeating the Constitutionalists and "pacifying" the country after their defeat, the occupying forces had rearmed, reorganized, and otherwise strengthened the Loyalist military and police forces and had disarmed and dissolved factions and organizations that supported the PRD.

With the pro-Balaguer faction exercising a monopoly on armed force and backed by U.S. Marines, compromises that had been negotiated by the OAS and García Godoy and incorporated into the document ending open hostilities were easily ignored. In the countryside and in lower-income districts of Santo Domingo, thousands of PRD activists were beaten and/or imprisoned during the electoral campaign, and several hundred were murdered. Many more were deported or fled into exile. Those who remained had good reason to be cautious. Bosch himself rarely made public appearances. His erstwhile colleagues in the leadership of the PRD, while conceding that Bosch probably would not have been allowed to assume the presidency under any circumstances, nevertheless continued to criticize him for failing to campaign.[21] After one of his bodyguards was killed, however, and his son was shot, he had good reason to fear for his life.

Trujillismo without Trujillo: The Rule of Balaguer

Even those who know Balaguer best describe him as enigmatic. Coming of age as a "nephew" of Trujillo,[22] aware of the dire consequences of inappropriate behavior, especially in public life, he learned to listen and not to speak unnecessarily, and to give away nothing unintentionally through facial expression or body language.

Balaguer has also been described as a pragmatist. Like Bosch, he was a writer and scholar; unlike Bosch, he was not notably restrained in the exercise of power either by temperament or by ideals and scruples.

21. J. Winston Arnaud G., acting secretary-general of the PRD, and Vicente Sanchez, president of the PRD, interviews with the author, Santo Domingo, January 10, 1985.
22. Actually a nephew of Trujillo's second wife. In the Dominican Republic, "nephew" often denotes a personal and/or political relationship rather than the literal familial one.

Finally, friends and enemies alike credit his intelligence and political acumen. Under the tutelage of Trujillo he had learned the fine arts of rewarding and disciplining supporters, coopting the uncommitted, and punishing his enemies. He also proved adept at combining authoritariansim with paternalism; he made sure that every public works project was presented as his personal contribution to the beneficiary community. He had the further advantage, of course, of ruling on behalf of the most powerful domestic and foreign interest groups, but he was no mere puppet. His overriding goal was maintaining his grip on power, and that he managed to do for a dozen years.

In consolidating his regime, Balaguer was able to build on the same power base that had sustained Trujillo: mainly the security forces, which in turn maintained tranquillity in the rural areas and delivered the peasant vote. To those who suffered imprisonment, exile, or worse, the Balaguer government seemed depressingly familiar—the survival of Trujillismo without Trujillo. Balaguer's supporters, however, saw his government as having begun the process of dismantling the Trujillo machine while avoiding the massive bloodletting that many had feared.

One of the first acts of the new PR government was the revision of the 1963 constitution. The country's twenty-fifth constitution was promulgated on November 28, 1966. Although, like most constitutions, it was democratic in form, it was more nearly authoritarian in substance than the one it superseded. Provisions in the 1963 constitution limiting foreign ownership of land and the size of landholdings were also revised.

Major tax benefits, guarantees, and other generous terms were offered to foreign capital. Low wages and a forcibly tamed labor force provided further incentives, and U.S. investors rushed to take advantage. New investment was particularly heavy in tourism, mineral extraction, sugar production, and light industry in the new "free trade zones."

Public assistance from the United States also flowed freely, as the Johnson administration sought to make the republic a model of the economic benefits of free enterprise and the now languishing Alliance for Progress. Combined economic and military assistance reached an all-time high of U.S. $111.6 million in fiscal year 1966, the fourth-highest sum extended to any Latin American country that year and the highest per capita extended to any country except Vietnam. Some 500 U.S. officials assumed technical assistance or other duties in the Dominican Republic. The level of assistance had dropped to U.S. $29.7 million by 1971, but it remained fourth highest in the hemisphere.[23]

The upshot of this heavy influx of aid and investment was an era of selective prosperity. By 1970, economists were speaking of the "Dominican miracle," related in both cause and character to the "Brazilian economic miracle" of the same period. In addition to the new sources of income for the middle and upper classes, as well as for the government itself, sugar prices had soared. But the new prosperity did not trickle down. While GNP growth rates and per capita income rose, the standard of living of the majority dipped even lower. Unemployment was chronic, at a level higher than 30 percent. Illiteracy and infant mortality remained high, and malnutrition was widespread.

In zones of rural unrest like the Cibao, where peasants had begun to occupy state lands (formerly communal lands that had been enclosed during the Trujillo era), Balaguer began a land-distribution program; the best lands, however, were generally claimed by military officers or others with political clout. Elsewhere, semifeudal land-tenure patterns, involving sharecropping or payment in kind for labor, remained intact.

Public works programs launched under Balaguer included the construction of irrigation canals, but these generally benefited large landholders rather than small ones. In 1972 a new agrarian reform law, drawn up by Vincho Castillo, was adopted. It provided that landowners who had benefited from government-sponsored irrigation were required to turn over a part of their land for redistribution to peasant families. The measure was fiercely resisted by landowners, however, and was poorly enforced. Castillo soon left the government because of the violence and corruption that accompanied the implementation of agrarian programs.[24]

Corruption, which had been rife under the Triumvirate, continued to have a prominent place in the government of Balaguer. By most accounts, Balaguer, unlike his notorious uncle, was not interested in

23. U.S. Agency for International Development, *U.S. Overseas Loans and Grants and Assistance from International Organizations; Obligations and Loan Authorizations, July 1, 1945–June 30, 1971* (Washington, DC: Government Printing Office, May 24, 1972).
24. Carlos Villaverde, director, Centro Dominicano de Estudios de la Educacion (CEDEE), interview with the author, Santo Domingo, January 8, 1985; Castillo, interview.

personal enrichment. But he used corruption, particularly of military officers, as a means of maintaining his power position.[25]

The political system over which President Balaguer presided after the withdrawal of the troops of the Inter-American Peace Force in September 1966 was sharply divided—charged, in fact, with all the bitterness of a feuding family. Nevertheless, the dependence of local government on the central power and the custom of winner-take-all lent great importance to supporting the winning presidential candidate. Moreover, Balaguer sought the collaboration of opposition party leaders, and he was able to draw upon the skills of leaders who had previously opposed him and would oppose him in the future.[26]

The leadership of the PRD and other left-of-center groups had been depleted through arrests and assassinations since the suppression of the 1965 rebellion. Bosch went into self-imposed exile in Europe. The remaining activist element of the PRD was rent by factionalism, while less committed former adherents defected to the Balaguer camp. But President Balaguer's attempts to reconcile and bring about consensus among the right-of-center forces were frustrated in 1967 by the meteoric rise of a new party on the far right.

The Quisqueyan Democratic party (PQD), purporting to follow the exiled Loyalist general, Elías Wessín y Wessín, attracted disaffected military officers and many of the former Trujillo collaborators who had not been absorbed by the Reformist party. Within 60 days of its founding, it had attained what was estimated to be the third-largest party membership in the country. Once established, however, it responded to the inevitable tendency to schism.

With little opposition in the 1968 municipal elections, the PR swept 66 of the 77 municipalities, receiving 649,765 of the total of 1,028,410 votes cast throughout the country. The PRD, the PQD, the UCN, and most other parties boycotted the elections. The Social Christian Revo-

25. According to Joaquín Ricardo, Balaguer's "nephew" and, as general secretary of the Partido Reformista Social Cristiano, would-be political heir, what was widely viewed as corruption was only favoritism (Joaquín Ricardo, interview with the author, Santo Domingo, January 11, 1985).
26. Two of the founders of the Social Christian party, for example, Alfonso Moreno Martínez and Guido D'Alessandro, accepted ambassadorships—Moreno Martínez to the United Nations and D'Alessandro to Venezuela. D'Alessandro subsequently served as minister of industry and commerce. Even Sacha Volman accepted a technical advisory position. Volman says that Peña Gómez was working for him at the time and negotiated with Balaguer over Volman's salary.

lutionary party (PRSC) participated, however, and with surprising results. Whereas in 1966 it had received only some 30,000 votes, in 1968 it received 124,719 and won control of two municipalities.

President Balaguer announced in December 1968 that all those who had been exiled for having fought in the 1965 civil war would be permitted to return. General Wessín wasted no time in accepting the invitation, but no word was heard from Colonel Francisco Caamaño Deñó, who had commanded the Constitutionalist forces. He had disappeared without a trace from his exile residence a year before, and many believed that he was dead.

Political violence, particularly assassinations claiming party leaders and other political figures on the left, continued throughout the late 1960s. It was intensified at the time of the visit of U.S. presidential envoy Governor Nelson Rockefeller, in 1969, and did not subside after his departure. This state of affairs led the bishop of Santiago and 53 priests to issue a pastoral letter condemning the government for its failure to protect "the right to work or even the right to live." And a commission led by a PRD senator charged at the United Nations that the murder of 362 members of the PRD since the end of the civil war was evidence that the government had resorted to political terrorism.[27]

By late 1969 it had become apparent that President Balaguer, without announcing his intentions, was campaigning for reelection. This resulted in a split in his own Reformist party, as the country's vice-president, Francisco Augusto Lora, with ambitions of his own, left the PR and accepted the candidacy offered by a new splinter party, the Movement for Democratic Integration against Reelection (MIDA).

The mayor of Santo Domingo, who was also chairman of the PR, publicly stated on December 2 that the prospect of Balaguer's candidacy for reelection was "the greatest obstacle to the Dominican People's choosing their destiny freely." Identical statements were issued simultaneously by spokesmen of the PRD, the PRSC, the MIDA, and a new center–right coalition, the Movement of National Conciliation. Engulfed by an internal dispute, the PQD did not join the other opposition parties in issuing this statement. Imbert Barrera had challenged Rear Admiral Lajara Burgos to a duel as a consequence of a controversy over the presidential nomination; Lajara Burgos was

---

27. *Quarterly Economic Review*, Nos. 3–4, 1969; No. 1, 1970.

unable to oblige because he was in New York. Meanwhile, General Wessín announced his candidacy.

Supported by the majority faction of the PR, President Balaguer on March 25 announced his candidacy for reelection. The PRD, expressing doubts that the government would allow itself to lose, decided to boycott the elections; other left-of-center parties followed suit. Parties to the right of center likewise threatened a boycott unless the president relinquished the powers of his office during the campaign. A compromise whereby Balaguer stepped down for a month before the election in favor of Ramón Ruiz Tejada, president of the Supreme Court, drew four of the reticent parties into the competition. Opposing Balaguer were Lora of the MIDA, Alfonso Moreno Martínez of the PRSC, General Wessín of the PQD, and Héctor García Godoy of the Movement of National Conciliation (MCN).

Political violence intensified in the months preceding the May 16 elections. As most of the victims were opponents of President Balaguer, opposition parties charged the police and the army, whose commander-in-chief had termed Balaguer's reelection a "national necessity," with responsibility. President Balaguer himself attributed the incidents to "uncontrollable forces." Into this highly charged atmosphere, Bosch returned on April 16 from his self-imposed exile. Clashes between his supporters and the police at the welcoming demonstrations for him resulted in four deaths, many injuries, and a large number of arrests.

As had been predicted, Balaguer was reelected on May 16, 1970, by a comfortable margin of 55.7 percent, leading his nearest rival, MIDA's Lora, by 305,038 votes. The PR carried all of the voting districts except one, Jarabacoa, the stronghold of General Wessín. The MIDA received 20.7 percent of the vote, deriving much of its strength from Santo Domingo, where it trailed by only 10,155 votes. The PQD's 13.2 percent of the vote came primarily from the rural areas. The PRSC polled 5 percent; and the MCN, whose initial candidate, García Godoy, died of natural causes 2 weeks before the election, polled only 4.4 percent. The PR also won 60 of the 74 seats in the Chamber of Deputies and all but one of the 27 Senate seats. All of the opposition parties charged electoral fraud; specific allegations included the waiver of the requirement of voting credentials for women, presumed to be more favorably disposed than men toward Balaguer, and the substitution of prepared ballot boxes for the authentic ones.

The PRD and other leftist parties that were boycotting the election claimed credit for the abstention of some 540,000, mostly urban, voters out of an electorate of approximately 1.7 million. Bosch had appealed to his followers through regular radio programs in Santo Domingo. After the elections, President Balaguer, asserting that "a democratic society has to resort to illegal and arbitrary measures if it is threatened by people seeking to bring about chaos," announced on June 12 that censorship of the radio had been introduced. The election was also followed by numerous arrests and dismissals from government service and further violence against Balaguer's political enemies.

Amnesty International reported in 1970 that a murdered body was appearing on the streets of Santo Domingo every 34 hours. At the end of the year the Santo Domingo newspaper *El Nacional* printed details of 186 political murders and 30 disappearances that had occurred during 1970 alone. The period between the election of Balaguer in 1966 and the end of 1971 witnessed well over 1000 political murders. It was calculated that there was a higher rate of political murder in the Dominican Republic in the years from 1969 through 1971 than in any comparable period under Trujillo. Not surprisingly, police brutality and torture were also commonplace.[28]

The president's hand was strengthened in July 1971 by the discovery of a conspiracy headed by General Wessín. President Balaguer gained political capital by placing General Wessín in front of television cameras and playing a recording of the general's voice announcing the fall of the government. General Wessín was turned over to the three commanders of the armed forces, who sent him into exile in Spain.

By late 1971 the incidence of violence had reached what most observers believed to be the high point since the 1965 civil war. Schools were closed, and Santo Domingo was said to resemble a ghost town as many preferred to stay off the streets. The principal perpetrators of the violence in this case were members of a group known as *La Banda* (The Band). They claimed to be private citizens sympathetic to the government and to have been systematically eliminating persons they considered its opponents. In fact, La Banda, like the "death squads" that were already terrorizing opponents of the dictatorships in Brazil and Guatemala and were soon to appear in other Latin American countries, was composed in part of army and police officers in civilian clothes. The archbishop protested that the church's pleas for

---

28. Herman and Brodhead, *Demonstration Elections*, pp. 47–48.

the respect of human rights had gone unheeded, and political leaders of both right and left charged that the group was working with the police.

In fact, it was commonly known that La Banda was operating under the direction of General Enrique Pérez y Pérez, commander of the National Police. Furthermore, as Balaguer was reputed to be in firm control of the security forces, it was assumed that he could put an end to the terrorism of La Banda if he chose to.[29] In October 1971, as charges and protests from both national and international quarters reached a crescendo, Balaguer publicly admonished the police to shoot only in self-defense and replaced General Pérez y Pérez with General Neit Nivar Seijas as commander of the National Police. By the end of the year, La Banda had been "disbanded," and the wave of violence had subsided.

The topic of primary concern to the politically articulate in 1972 was the prospect of Balaguer's candidacy for a third term. Although the next presidential election was not scheduled until 1974, opposition parties and opponents of President Balaguer within his own party charged that he was already campaigning and taking actions against prospective opponents in preparation for his reelection. Once again, the major parties had been discussing the establishment of a common front to boycott the elections if Balaguer offered himself as a candidate. The PRD, having been deserted by most of the parties to an early boycott agreement in 1970, was hesitant, but in October 1972 it was announced that leaders of the PRD, PQD, and MIDA had signed such an agreement. The PRSC had also indicated interest in the boycott plan.

The PRD was still considered to be by far the strongest of the opposition parties, although since 1963 it had suffered a continual depletion of its leaders, through assassination, exile, and imprisonment, and, like all other parties, it suffered from internal schisms.

---

29. Even Balaguer's close friend Vincho Castillo says that Balaguer could have reined in Pérez y Pérez and La Banda had he chosen to (Castillo, interview). Some Dominican leaders, however, believe that Balaguer's control over the military and police was considerably less than complete, given the propensity of U.S. agencies and officials to use the Dominican security forces for their own purposes. Alfonso Moreno Martínez discloses that in 1971 a Dominican businessman closely linked to the military hierarchy told him that the military was going to "shoot all the communists." If Balaguer did not go along, the businessman said, they would shoot him, too (Moreno Martínez, interview).

Bosch's advocacy, after the 1970 elections, of "dictatorship with popular support" had been rejected by most other party leaders.

The MIDA had essentially the same social base of support as the trunk group of the PR, except that it was stronger in urban than in rural areas; its raison d'être continued to be prevention of the *continuismo* of Balaguer, but it lacked a leader of sufficient popularity to challenge him effectively. The PQD continued to attract military leaders and others whose status had depreciated since the assassination of Trujillo or the fall of the Triumvirate, but it was handicapped in 1972 by the fact that its leader, General Wessín, was in exile.

The year 1973 brought more disaster and diversion for what had been the Constitutionalist movement. On February 3, the mystery of the whereabouts of Colonel Caamaño was solved. Leading a small guerrilla group—10 men in all—who had been living in Cuba, Caamaño landed on the beach at Caracoles in the Bay of Ocoa and moved into the nearby mountains. An army First Brigade unit of some 2000 troops found the group after about 2 weeks. Caamaño was wounded in a shootout and, 5 hours later, was shot to death while a prisoner. Six of his companions were killed—most while in captivity—and two of the survivors were soon captured; they were detained for several months, then sent into exile. The colonel's nephew, First Lieutenant Claudio Caamaño Grullón, escaped into the mountains where he remained for almost 2 months. When he emerged from hiding and came down from the mountains, it was under the protection of a bishop who was then acting head of the Dominican Catholic Church. The younger Caamaño took refuge in the Mexican Embassy on April 16 and later went into exile in Mexico.

On the occasion of the landing, Balaguer had declared a state of emergency, closing radio and television stations and newspaper offices, sending troops to occupy the university and patrol city streets, and detaining some 1400 political, labor, and student leaders. Balaguer accused Bosch and other PRD leaders of complicity and of planning a mass urban uprising.

Claudio Caamaño has said that, in fact, no urban uprising was planned or anticipated. Rather, the guerrilla group had envisioned a long-term campaign centered in the mountains. The invasion plan had not been shared with Dominican Communists nor with the PRD leadership. It was supported, however, by some elements of the

3. CONTEMPORARY HISTORY

PRD, and by a number of nonpartisan Dominicans, including some bankers.[30]

Later in the year, Bosch, outvoted by a PRD majority on the issue of participation in the 1974 elections, withdrew from the party and founded another, the Dominican Liberation party (PLD). The PRD, which remained under the leadership of Peña Gómez, proceeded in early 1974 to nominate Antonio Guzmán, a wealthy rancher, as its presidential candidate. It soon became very clear however, that Balaguer would brook no serious opposition. The armed forces were openly intimidating political leaders and would-be voters. Barracks throughout the country looked like PR headquarters, and soldiers carried PR flags at the ends of their bayonets.[31] Although there is no evidence that Balaguer was aware of it, some military officers even conspired, as the 1974 elections approached, to assassinate Peña Gómez.[32]

After this resurgence of terrorism, which the electoral council refused to recognize, the PRD and most other parties withdrew their candidates. Only the small Popular Democratic party (PDP) stayed in the race. Balaguer won by a margin of 85 percent, but only half of the 2 million registered voters bothered to turn out.

As Balaguer began his fourth term, the energy crisis took its toll on the Dominican economy. Unemployment became even more severe, while inflation mounted, shattering the security of the middle class. Corruption, particularly in the military, also became a major issue, and Balaguer, aging and almost blind, was no longer able to make optimum use of the resources at his command.

30. Claudio Caamaño, interview. Caamaño now lives on the outskirts of Santo Domingo, where he breeds tropical fish.
31. Sánchez and Arnaud, interviews.
32. On an evening shortly before the 1974 election, representatives of several parties met at the home of the acting president of the Quisqueyan party to decide whether or not to boycott the elections. There Peña Gómez received word that elements of the military were planning to surround the house and assassinate him that very evening. With that information he left the house immediately with Guido D'Alessandro, on the pretense of having to attend a meeting elsewhere. D'Alessandro drove a zigzag course around Santo Domingo until he was convinced that they were not being followed. He then took Peña Gómez to the home of his brother's girlfriend, and later to the Italian Embassy, where, unbeknown to the ambassador, Peña Gómez stayed for several days (Guido D'Alessandro, PRSC leader, interviews with the author, Boca Chica and Santo Domingo, January 4, 11, and 13, 1985).

A Pivotal Election

As the 1978 elections approached, it was clear that Balaguer's control was slipping. Apart from the downturn in the economy, the most important change in the political environment had been the new concern in the U.S. Congress for the protection of human rights and the embracing of that theme by U.S. president Jimmy Carter, who took office at the beginning of 1977. In preparation for the election, Balaguer allowed the long-banned Dominican Communist party (PCD) to register—ostensibly a liberal gesture, but one that was expected to draw votes from the PRD, benefiting the PR. Convinced that his election would have to appear to be fair, Balaguer also invited the OAS to send a delegation of observers.

On election day, May 16, 1978, polling proceeded without incident, but as the vote tallying got under way, the results being broadcast on radio and television, it became clear that the PRD was building a strong lead. At about 4:00 a.m. on May 17, troops occupied the headquarters of the Central Election Board (JCE) and most of the country's polling places. They also took over radio and television stations and began to broadcast music, interspersed with a recorded message from the armed forces minister, General Juan René Beauchamp Javier, which described the electoral situation as "normal" and said that no coup had taken place.

The PRD, anticipating support this time from erstwhile domestic and foreign opponents of unmanaged elections, decided against staging demonstrations or other forms of mass action. Support was soon forthcoming, particularly in the form of newspaper advertisements, from unfamiliar quarters: the Church hierarchy; organizations of domestic and foreign businessmen, industrialists, and professionals; leaders of Santiago's aristocracy; and even some political leaders of the PR; along with the predictable support from universities, labor organizatons, and most political parties.

Officials of the U.S. government, in contact with former Ecuadorian president Galo Plaza, head of the OAS delegation, also swung into action. The U.S. defense attaché arrived at the office of General Beauchamp at 7:00 a.m. on May 17. Kept waiting until the following morning, the attaché was finally able to tell the general that a coup or corruption of the electoral process would have grave consequences for U.S.–Dominican relations. He stressed that on this occasion military and civilian arms of the U.S. government were speaking with one voice. Frustrated in his attempts to see Balaguer, U.S. Ambassador Robert L. Yost visited the foreign minister, Admiral Jiménez, and delivered a similar message. Two days later, President Carter issued a public warning that future U.S. support for the Dominican government would depend on respect for the integrity of the elections. Meanwhile, Galo Plaza had spoken with Balaguer, and protests and warnings had been cabled from many European and Latin American countries, notably including Venezuela, supplier of the republic's petroleum products.[33]

Vote counting resumed on May 18, but was halted again as troops occupied municipal buildings throughout the country. A number of PRD members were arrested. That evening, Balaguer broke his silence and addressed a nationwide television audience, but his message was ambiguous and less than reassuring. He urged that election results be respected, but at the same time he charged the PRD with electoral fraud and denounced foreign interference. Nevertheless, Balaguer issued instructions that night to Beauchamp and to National Police Chief Neit Nivar Seijas to withdraw their forces. The counting resumed, unhindered, 4 days later. It was not until the end of May, however, that the JCE produced provisional figures for the presidential contest, showing Guzmán with 832,647 votes to 682,850 for the Balaguer, and the skirmish, at that point, was far from over.

If Balaguer's military and civilian supporters had decided to concede the presidency to the PRD, they had not yet decided under what conditions they would do so. PRD and PR leaders continued to debate publicly and to confer privately. Reformistas repeated the familiar charge that PRD caudillo Peña Gómez was a dangerous pro-communist. They also charged electoral fraud and called for new elections. Manuel Joaquín Castillo, president of the JCF, although a Balaguer appointee, refused to corroborate charges of electoral fraud and was removed from office.

Finally, on July 7, the official results of the vote count were released. The JCE, demonstrating an attitude toward impartiality that had been commonplace over the past dozen years, made the absurd decision to count votes that had *not* been cast in some provinces and to divide them evenly between the top two parties. That deprived the PRD of one seat in the Chamber of Deputies and four in the Senate that

33. G. Pope Atkins, *Arms and Politics in the Dominican Republic* (Boulder, CO: Westview Press, 1981), pp. 104–107.

provisional results showed it to have won. As a consequence, the PR maintained its majority in the Senate, where it was able to block many of the initiatives of the incoming government.[34] Meanwhile, Peña Gómez left the country for an extended period of foreign travel.[35]

As a parting insult to the nation, the lame-duck, PR-dominated Congress, in extraordinary session, passed legislation extending various advantages to themselves and their friends. These included big pay raises for the armed forces and police and measures limiting civilian control over those forces.

The PRD, under President Antonio Guzmán, returned to power in August 1978, after suffering 15 years of terror and deceit. Guzmán opened up the system, eliminating restraints on civil liberties and urging respect for human rights. He also sought limited controls on foreign investment and introduced measures intended to benefit the poor. But the PRD of the late 1970s lacked the inspiration and optimism of its youth; it was moderated, subdued, cautious.

---

34. Vincho Castillo, who headed the investigation of charges of fraud brought by the PR, says that he uncovered such fraud on a large scale. He found, for example, that many who had voted in 1974, when Balaguer ran almost uncontested, were turned away from the polls in 1978. He says that he had supported the *reformista* call for new elections but that the compromise solution, supported by Carter and by Carlos Andres Pérez of Venezuela and accepted by Sonia Guzmán, negotiating on behalf of her father, was that the PRD would give up the Senate.

    PRD leaders do not confirm accounts that a deal was struck. Party president Vicente Sánchez, who managed Guzmán's campaign, says that Guzmán simply was not in a position to counter the actions of the JCE, as the confirmation of his own victory hung in the balance. He believes the PR insisted on maintaining control of the Senate in order to control judgeships and thus prevent convictions on charges of corruption.
35. It appears that Peña Gómez left the country in order to facilitate the transition to PRD rule, but there were also reports that his life had again been threatened.

4
SOCIAL AND ECONOMIC STRUCTURES

Race and Social Stratification

The Dominican population is sharply stratified by race and class. In the early 1980s, the wealthiest 6 percent of the population disposed of about 43 percent of total national income, while the poorest 50 percent shared only 13 percent of that income.[1] Racial distinctions are hardly clear-cut, but the population is said to be about 16 percent white, 11 percent black, and 73 percent mulatto. There is also a small number of Orientals, but scarcely a trace remains of the indigenous Arawak population. Though racial discrimination has never been so extreme in the Dominican Republic as was the case until recently in the southern United States there is no mistaking the gradations of color from dark to light as one moves up the socioeconomic pyramid.

The Gentry and the New Rich

Members of the white upper class are in large part descendants of Spaniards, who came in several waves between 1492 and the Spanish recolonization of the 1860s. The earliest settlers were largely from Andalusia. Canary Islanders predominated in the later wave of immigration that began in the 1680s, while those left behind after the second Spanish withdrawal in 1865 were largely from Catalonia. The Spaniards implanted their language, religion, and culture; most subsequent im-

---

1. Howard J. Wiarda and Michael J. Kryzanek, *The Dominican Republic: A Caribbean Crucible* (Boulder, CO: Westview Press, 1982), p. 52.

migrants, particularly the large number of Italians and Maronite Christians from the Middle East who arrived between the 1870s and World War I, were assimilated.[2]

The early Spanish settlers hardly constituted an aristocracy. They were not wealthy, even by the standards of their time. But many did hold land and, until 1822, slaves, and they were highly race conscious. Later immigrants from Spain and other parts of Europe tended to be less conscious of race. Men who arrived without families cohabitated with black women, giving rise to a predominantly mulatto population.

The beginnings of an aristocracy were to be found in the Cibao region in the later part of the nineteenth century. Refugees from Cuba's long independence struggle, many of them highly skilled, settled in that region, intermarried with the white Dominican landowning class there, and built a thriving economy based on the export of tobacco. They also established Santiago as the country's cultural capital.

Other Cuban refugees settled farther south, in the vicinity of Santo Domingo, where the terrain was more suitable for growing sugarcane. The sugar industry continued to prosper after the tobacco trade declined, and Santo Domingo salvaged its position as the nation's commercial and financial as well as political center. Nevertheless, Santiago maintained the reputation, and to some degree the power, represented in its full name, Santiago de los Caballeros (Santiago of the Gentlemen). Members of the Santiago aristocracy have continued to be prominent in public life.[3]

Traditional landowning families, from Santiago and elsewhere, have established interests in business and industry to complement their agricultural interests. But new layers of economic elites have emerged with each period of sustained economic boom. Thus there is an industrial and commercial elite that came into being during the Trujillo years and an even newer rich class—in light industry, banking, and tourism, for example—that emerged during the 1970s. The newer elites include military officers and their families, who profited from questionable dealings and outright corruption.

---

2. Immigration to the Dominican Republic has been continuous in the twentieth century. One group of settlers that, although largely assimilated, maintains its identity, is the group of Jewish refugees from Hitler's Germany who settled at Sosua, on the north coast, in 1940.
3. Ian Bell, *The Dominican Republic* (Boulder, CO: Westview Press, 1981), pp. 112–125.

4. SOCIAL AND ECONOMIC STRUCTURES

Economic elites, both old and new, made enormous gains in wealth and power during the Balaguer years, as the gap between rich and poor became a grand canyon. Eschewing formal channels and structures of business and government, these elites normally pursue their interests by taking advantage of networks of family and personal ties. Their perspectives extend well beyond the national society, as their wealth derives directly or indirectly from international trade and investment and their taste runs to imported goods and cultural trends. Political arrangements among elite groups are generally reached in private, in country clubs or men's clubs or other gathering places of the wealthy.

The Middle Sector

The expansion of government and commerce, beginning during the Trujillo era, has generated an enormous increase in professional and white-collar jobs. The middle sector now constitutes some 15 to 20 percent of the population, and its influence is increasing in politics as well as in the economy. This sector, drawing upon electoral support from, and the potential disruptiveness of, mobilized elements of the working and would-be working classes, has given substance to the rituals of the electoral and parliamentary systems and has been the prime beneficiary of the trappings of modern government.

The Dominican middle sector does not constitute an intermediate level of property holders. Nor do its representatives have other independent sources of wealth. Rather, it is a salaried sector, dependent on the continuous expansion of commerce and government. Thus it is, on the whole, highly insecure in both income and status, and its political behavior tends to be erratic compared to the behavior either of elites or of manual laborers.

Representatives of the sector who occupy the leading roles in government and other social institutions, as well as managerial roles in business, tend to be white or nearly white, whereas mulattoes of darker hues occupy middle- and lower-income and status roles within the sector. Exceptions to this rule are found in the military and in electoral politics. As has been rule in many other countries, the armed forces and electoral politics have constituted avenues for the social mobility of poorer and darker individuals. Electoral politics, however, as substance rather than fraud, has a short history. The road to power has generally run through the military, and it is no coincidence that the

Dominican Republic has had more black and mulatto presidents than any other nation in the Hispanic world.[4]

Though the lower margins of the middle sector are not easy to delineate, this sector generally differs in attitudes and behavior patterns, as well as in occupations and income levels, from the massive lower class. Members of the middle sector tend to be ambitious and pretentious, adopting to the extent income allows the tastes and styles of the rich. They enjoy greater family stability than is common in the lower class, and they are highly conscious of family background and of race and color. Unlike the elites, however, most members of this sector cannot afford to be addicted to imported goods; therefore, they constitute the domestic market for the products of domestic light industry.

The Poor Majority

The relative affluence of the Dominican upper and middle classes is built upon the abject poverty of some 75 to 80 percent of the population. This deprived majority is mulatto and black, its black antecedents having come directly from Africa as slaves or in later migrations from Haiti, the British West Indies, and the U.S. mainland.[5] Most Dominicans are undernourished. A study released by the Dominican Planning Agency in 1978 indicated that the diets of 75 percent of the population were inadequate and that 50 percent had seriously deficient diets.[6] Only 55 percent of the population has access to safe water. Chronic unemployment affects about one-fourth of the labor force, and half the force is generally underemployed. In early 1985 unemployment was running higher than 30 percent.

In the shantytowns that surround Santo Domingo, the tiny makeshift houses of wood and tin typically lack electricity and running

---

4. Wiarda and Kryzanek, *Dominican Republic*.
5. The Anglican church, established by immigrants from the British West Indies, is still strong in several areas, particularly along the eastern coast. Services are now conducted mainly in Spanish, however. In the area of San Pedro de Macorís, on the southern coast, east of Santo Domingo, descendants of runaway slaves from the United States maintain some of their distinct customs (Bishop Telésforo A. Isaac, head of the Dominican Anglican church, interview with the author, Puerto Plata, January 12, 1985).
6. Robert W. Mashek and Stephen G. Vetter, *La Fundación Interamericana en la Republica Dominicana una decada de apoyo a las organizaciones de desarrollo locales* (Rosslyn, VA: Fundación Interamericana, 1983), p. 14.

water. Open sewers spread disease among children already weakened by malnutrition. As peasants escaping the even more dismal rural areas swelled the ranks of the urban poor in the 1970s, housing and services deteriorated even further.

Urban poverty, juxtaposed against ostentatious wealth, has been a cause of embarrassment and occasionally of fear for some upper- and middle-class Dominicans. The urban poor have been the PRD's most reliable base of support. They fought and died for the Constitutionalists in 1965, but, in 1984–1985, even they rioted over price increases for staple commodities imposed by a PRD government. The rural poor have not resorted to violence on any significant scale since the U.S. occupation in the 1920s, but their desperation has been expressed in massive migration, first to provincial towns, then on to the larger cities. Such migration generally results in the atomization of families.

The rural poor typically live in tiny houses of mud and thatch or wood or in the barren field camps *(bateyes)* of the sugar plantations. Services and social amenities are virtually nonexistent. Only 4 of the country's 12 hospitals with more than 300 beds are outside of Santo Domingo. Despite the efforts of government and development agencies, clinics and schools remain few and far between.[7] About 80 percent of the rural population is illiterate, and rural unemployment sometimes runs as high as 50 percent. Life expectancy, at 62 years for the nation as a whole, is 10 years shorter in rural areas.

Arable land is scarce and highly concentrated; 75 percent of the farmers hold less than 15 percent of the land. It is also poorly managed. Production per hectare is among the lowest in Latin America. Wealthy landowners keep much of their fertile land as pasture, producing beef for export or for the 4 percent of the domestic population who can afford it.[8] Landholdings that are not highly concentrated are instead highly fragmented in *minifundios*. There is almost no middle ground. Most peasants are landless or own plots too small or barren to feed a family.

Those who find work on large plantations may earn the rural minimum wage—5 pesos daily in early 1985 (considerably less than the urban minimum of 175 pesos monthly, or about 8.75 daily),[9] but

---

7. Carlos Villaverde, interview with the author, Santo Domingo, January 8, 1985.
8. Noam Chomsky and Edward S. Herman, *The Washington Connection and Third World Fascism* (Boston: South End Press, 1979), p. 251.
9. The peso was pegged at about 3 to $1 on the parallel market during most of 1984. In February 1985, the official peso–dollar parity was eliminated entirely, and the parallel rate became official.

generally for no more than 6 months of the year. Most landowners hire fewer than 10 field hands and thus are not bound by minimum wage or other labor legislation. Even the government is generally guilty of paying less than the minimum wage to the mostly Haitian cane cutters on its sugar plantations.[10]

Most peasants, whether they work for themselves or for a patron, have no old-age pensions and no protection against unemployment, crop failure, natural disaster, or disability. Government-sponsored crop insurance became available in 1984, but only for sizable crops. Rural unions are rare, and where they exist, they are even weaker than their urban counterparts. Strikes on the major plantations have often been broken by the police or the armed forces.

Land-reform measures legislated by the short-lived Bosch government were weakened by the government of Balaguer, and even the limited reforms sought by Balaguer were fiercely opposed by landowners. The Dominican Agrarian Institute, established in 1962, had distributed land from state holdings to about 67,000 families by 1980, but that achievement was dwarfed by the needs of almost 500,000 rural families. Furthermore, the land distributed to peasants was generally of low productivity. The best parcels had been acquired by military officers and other government officials.

In general, the distribution of land to peasant families was not accompanied by the extension of credit or technical assistance. An agrarian bank was established to make loans to small farmers, but it was undercapitalized and could not begin to meet the needs. Meanwhile, the prices of imported seed and fertilizers have soared as the peso has been devalued.[11]

At the bottom of the social and economic heap are the Haitian laborers. Since 1952, bilateral agreements between the Dominican and Haitian governments have regulated the importation of Haitian cane cutters for employment on the large state-owned sugar plantations, generally for 6-month periods. About 20,000 cross into the Dominican Republic each year legally, but it is estimated that another 60,000 cross each year illegally. These Haitians have no civil rights and often work in conditions bordering on slavery. Like Mexican workers in the

---

10. Yvette Sabbagh, sociologist, Centro de Estudios de la Realidad Social Dominicana (CERESD), Universidad Autónoma de Santo Domingo (UASD), interview with the author, Santo Domingo, January 7, 1985.
11. Villaverde, interview.

4. SOCIAL AND ECONOMIC STRUCTURES

United States, the Haitians become scapegoats when the economy fails, and there are widespread popular demands to block their entry or to expel those who have settled in the Dominican Republic.

Demographic Trends

The Dominican population is fast-growing and young. Despite an average national life expectancy of only 62 years and an infant mortality rate of 73 per 1000, the country's annual population growth rate has been quite high. Estimates for the 1960s ranged from 2.9 percent to 3.5 percent. By 1981 the rate had dropped to 2.4 percent. Still, rural families had an average of six children each, and almost half of the national population was younger than 15.[12]

The national population, about 6.3 million in the mid 1980s, was only 3 million in 1960. Then the population was predominantly rural, but the ratio of urban to total population increased from 30 percent to 54 percent between 1960 and 1980. Santo Domingo, with 1.3 million inhabitants, accounts for about one-fifth of the national population. Santiago, in the fertile valley of the Cibao, is the second-largest city, with 400,000 residents.

For unhappy reasons, Dominicans are a people on the move. Rural–urban migration began in earnest in the 1930s and has steadily gathered momentum. Landless peasants, fleeing the hopelessness and boredom of the countryside, make their ways first to the nearest town and ultimately to one of the larger cities, mainly Santo Domingo. Working-class families who have been in the cities and towns for several generations are outnumbered now by newcomers from the countryside.

Few, however, find their fortunes in the cities. City dwellers also find opportunities scarce, and professionals and workers alike emigrate in large numbers, particularly to Puerto Rico and to the U.S. mainland. It has been estimated that by the mid 1980s, 800,000 Dominicans had migrated to the United States. At least half of them were in New York City; another 200,000 or so were in San Juan. Meanwhile, from neighboring Haiti, where economic conditions are even worse, desperate workers, documented or otherwise, continue to pour over

---

12. Paul B. Goodwin, Jr. (ed.), *Global Studies: Latin America* (Guilford, CT: Dushkin Publishing Group, 1984), pp. 176–177.

the borders into the Dominican Republic. Their numbers were estimated at 200,000 in 1983.

Migration is an important factor, but only one of several factors that cause instability in the family unit among the poor majority of Dominicans. Common-law unions have long been the rule rather than the exception, particularly in rural areas. Marriages may be civil or religious or both, but priests are scarce in rural areas and civil marriages would require at least two trips to the nearest town. Since legal questions are likely to arise only when property is involved, the 75 to 80 percent of the population who have virtually no property have little incentive to formalize their unions. These unions may nevertheless be permanent, and several decades ago, family relationships in rural areas were more stable than those in cities. But that is no longer the case. The push from the countryside and the pull of the town affect both men and women. Men may be the first to leave, but young women with children to support also must seek jobs; the children may be left behind with grandparents until they, too, are old enough to go to town.

It is estimated that only 20 percent of all cohabiting couples in the Dominican Republic are legally married.[13] Among the poor, cohabitation, whether or not it involves marriage, is often temporary. Many households are headed by women; mothers provide continuity for their children, who may have different fathers. Within the past decade, upper- and middle-class women have made considerable progress in integrating business and the professions, and they have begun to assert themselves politically as well. Lower-class women, however, continue to have enormous responsibility without authority.

Economic Growth and Diversification

The Dominican economy has suffered in exaggerated form from the problems of uncertainty and dependency and from the deterioration in the terms of trade for producers of primary products that have plagued the Third World generally and Latin America in particular. Sugarcane cultivation was introduced to the island by Columbus himself, and the problem of the concentration of landholdings on the one hand and increasing landlessness on the other dates from the arrival of the

13. Bell, *Dominican Republic*, pp. 130–132.

4. SOCIAL AND ECONOMIC STRUCTURES

earliest settlers. Nevertheless, the republic's economy was based essentially on subsistence agriculture until the Trujillo era. Trujillo transformed the economy for his personal advantage and coincidentally left behind an export-oriented economy heavily dependent on sugar. Sugar dependency has put the economy on a roller coaster, reaching occasional highs of prosperity only to plunge once against to depths of debt and depression.

Economic growth since the early 1960s has been erratic but substantial. Between 1960 and 1980, real per capita income rose from $513 to $1050, while gross domestic product rose from $1.8 billion to $5.7 billion.[14] After 1980, the Dominican economy, along with that of the United States and much of the rest of the Western world, slipped into recession.

Growth has generally come in spurts. There was a spurt in the late 1960s, induced largely by U.S. aid and investment, as the U.S. government sought to show that its military intervention had been beneficial and U.S. investors rushed to take advantage of new incentives. The average of 5 percent annual growth in the 1970s represents a leveling of the peak of 9 to 10 percent growth in 1974–1975, resulting from high sugar prices, and the trough of 1978 when low sugar prices and the soaring cost of imported oil combined to produce economic decline. The price of sugar has continued to sink in the 1980s. From a high of 76 cents a pound in 1975, it had dropped by 1984 to about 6 cents a pound, less than half the cost of production.[15]

All governments since the early 1960s have sought to diminish the country's dependence on sugar, and considerable diversification has taken place, both within the basket of agricultural exports and in the economy as a whole. Sugar declined, during the 1970s, from 48 percent to 35 percent of all exports; while exports of coffee, cocoa, and tobacco increased to account for about 30 percent. Perhaps more important, under the Guzmán government, in 1979, the country became self-sufficient, for the first time, in rice and beans, the staples of the Dominican diet. The Guzmán government had placed a high priority on the expansion of food production for domestic consumption and the retardation of migration from the countryside to the cities. That self-sufficiency was only temporary, however. The country is gener-

---

14. Mashek and Vetter, *La Fundacion Interamericana*, p. 13.
15. Roger Lowenstein, "Gulf and Western Pullout Stuns Dominicans," *Wall Street Journal*, June 18, 1984, p. 26.

ally close to self-sufficiency in rice, but remains, in most years, a net importer of beans.[16]

Almost half of the work force was still in agriculture in the early 1980s, but agricultural output had declined in the previous two decades from 26 percent to 17 percent of the gross domestic product. Governments had consistently given priority to industrialization, and manufacturing had grown from less than 1 percent of GDP to 18 percent. Industrial growth was particularly notable in sugar refining, textiles, pharmaceuticals, and cement. Exports from the light industrial sector now account for up to one-fourth of the country's foreign-exchange earnings. New government agencies have been created to finance industrial development and to seek new markets for Dominican products.

Mining has also of late become an important activity. After the obscene clamor for gold by the conquistadores and early settlers, the islands' mineral resources were virtually ignored until the last few years of Trujillo's reign. The exportation of bauxite was begun in the late 1950s, but it was not until the late 1960s that nickel became an important export. The country's newest mineral export—newest, that is, since it was last exported in the 1520— is gold. Gold, in alloy with silver, has been exported since 1975. At the beginning of 1980, gold, or *doré*, as the alloy is known, became the republic's most valuable export, but the gold market weakened later in the year. Nevertheless, mining, led by ferronickel, continued to account for about one-fourth of total exports.

Tourism is another of the country's booming new industries. Until the 1970s, tourism was scarcely significant as a source of foreign exchange, but during that decade the number of tourists visiting annually more than tripled, rising to about half a million. The tourist industry has generated thousands of jobs, though mostly low-paying ones, and has had important spinoffs for construction and other industries. It has also spurred government investment in infrastructure, particularly in the construction of roads and airports and the modernization of the old center city of Santo Domingo and the old port, Puerto Plata, on the north coast. A government agency, INFRATUR, created in 1971, supervises expenditures related to the promotion of tourism. President Guzmán created a new cabinet position for the oversight of

---

16. Marion Ford, agriculture officer, U.S. Agency for International Development, interview with the author, Santo Domingo, January 8, 1985.

tourism, and the Jorge Blanco government has made the promotion of tourism one of its highest priorities.

As has been mentioned, the new prosperity of the 1970s was narrowly distributed. It made the old rich richer, created new categories of new rich, and expanded the middle class, but it did not trickle down to the poverty-stricken majority. This was in part a consequence of policy decisions rather than of policy failures. For the large contingent of state employees, wages and salaries were frozen by government edict. For most other categories of workers, wages were depressed as a consequence of high levels of unemployment and the repression of organized labor.

Much of the new industry was capital intensive, so the number of new jobs created was not nearly equal to the number of would-be workers entering the labor force. Furthermore, rapid economic growth generated inflation. The single- and double-digit levels of inflation the country has experienced in recent years seem mild compared to the triple-digit inflation experienced in some other Latin American countries, but such inflation was devastating to those whose wages were frozen, not to mention to the half of the population that was unemployed or underemployed. Moreover, with the introduction in the early 1980s, at the behest of the IMF, of the floating parallel rate of exchange for the peso, inflation mounted rapidly. It was officially pegged at 34 percent for 1984, but government calculations underestimated the real burden of inflation.[17]

Finally, the system of taxation did nothing to redress imbalances; in fact, it made things worse. Personal income taxes, ranging from 2 percent on salaries to 10 percent on real estate earnings, are among the lowest in the hemisphere, and only a fraction of those eligible actually pay. Corporate taxes range from 10 percent to 49.4 percent, but both personal and corporate tax laws are full of loopholes. Income taxes account for no more than one-fourth of the total tax burden. The remainder are import and export levies, excise taxes, license fees, and, since 1983, value-added taxes—all taxes that are ultimately passed on to the consumer. Furthermore, citizens who can afford to do so pay in other ways—for example, private schools, private security guards—to compensate for the inadequacy of public services.

17. U.S. Embassy, Santo Domingo, *The Dominican Republic: Investment Climate Report*, December 1984.

Dependency and Development

The growth and modernization of the Dominican economy since the 1960s have been impressive, but such growth and modernization have been largely fueled and controlled by foreign—mainly U.S.— companies and by U.S. markets and suppliers. The United States supplies about half of the republic's imports and purchases about two-thirds of its exports. It follows that the republic's options have been severely limited and that factors other than the public interest and welfare of Dominicans have often governed economic decision making.

The Dominican economy was already linked to that of the United States through trade and U.S. loans and investments before the turn of the century, and the links were drawn tighter during and after the U.S. occupation of 1916–1924. But the new wave of U.S. investment dates from the mid to late 1960s when constitutional obstacles, including limitations on the foreign ownership of land, were removed or modified; labor was pacified; a range of incentives were offered to investors by both Dominican and U.S. governments; and U.S. public assistance financed infrastructure projects that were helpful to business.

Foreign investment has been heaviest in agribusiness and food processing but has also increased sharply in mining, tourism, light industry, banking, insurance, and real estate. In the early 1980s there were some 125 subsidiaries of U.S. firms operating in the Dominican Republic, many of them in one of the country's four tax-free zones.[18] Many more U.S. investors have small business holdings. The U.S.-based corporations accounted for about two-thirds of the total registered foreign investment, Canadian-based ones for about one-fourth. (Falconbridge, owner of the nickel mine at Bonao and thus the second-largest private investor in the republic, is registered in Canada but its major shareholders are U.S. based.) The only other country having a high level of investment was Great Britain. Among U.S. firms, the heaviest investors were Exxon, Texaco, Citibank, GTE, Atlantic Richfield, Colgate-Palmolive, Wometco, Philip Morris, and,

---

18. The U.S.-based owner of a factory in one of the tax-free zones, who asked not to be identified, said that his Dominican operations were 20 percent more productive than similar operations in the Far East. His workers' base pay was 40 pesos a week (about $2 a day). They could earn up to another 140 pesos a week in piecework, but piecework pay carried no fringe benefits. The fuzzy toys made in his factory were sold to a Norwegian cruise liner for $8–10 a dozen. They retailed on the cruise liner for $8–10 each.

4. SOCIAL AND ECONOMIC STRUCTURES

until January 1985, the giant among U.S. multinationals, Gulf and Western.[19]

Gulf and Western had more than $200 million invested in some 90 businesses in the Dominican Republic. It was the country's largest private landowner, with about 8 percent of all arable land, and its largest employer. The centerpiece of Gulf and Western's Dominican empire was the sugar plantations and refinery complex—the country's largest—at La Romana, which Gulf and Western acquired from the South Puerto Rico Sugar Company in 1967.

Gulf and Western also maintained a 350-room seaside resort at La Romana. In 1969 Gulf and Western took over management of a large tax-free zone adjacent to its Cajuiles golf course. Foreign companies settling within the zone enjoy duty-free import and export privileges and a 10-year tax-free status. The zone is surrounded by a high fence topped with barbed wire, and its entrances are guarded by National Police as well as customs agents. U.S. AFL-CIO officials who visited the zone in the late 1970s said it had the air of a "modern slave-labor camp." They believed its controlled access was designed primarily to thwart labor organization efforts. In fact, an organizing effort in the mid 1970s had been broken by police and troops armed with submachine guns.[20]

Global annual sales of Gulf and Western are larger than the GNP of the Dominican Republic, and the Dominican government was left in a poor bargaining position when it came to the mobilization of professional manpower and influence. The company cultivated good relations with military and police officials, relations that were useful in maintaining labor peace. It was accused of employing repressive tactics against labor leaders and political antagonists and of outright bribery. It had been engaged in a running dispute with PRD governments since 1978 over tax evasion and other irregularities in which the Balaguer administration allegedly connived.[21] Even the U.S. Securities and Exchanges Commission (SEC) alleged that Gulf and Western withheld millions of dollars it owed to the Dominican government,[22] that it made "questionable" payments through foreign subsidiaries,

---

19. Tom Barry, Beth Wood, and Deb Preusch, *The Other Side of Paradise: Foreign Control in the Caribbean* (New York: Grove Press, 1984), p. 297.
20. Chomsky and Herman, *Washington Connection*, pp. 246-249.
21. Bell, *Dominican Republic*, p. 368.
22. Wiarda and Kryzanek, *Dominican Republic*, p. 78.

and that it entered into a secret agreement with Dominican government officials to speculate in sugar.[23]

Thus, Gulf and Western was an obvious target for nationalistic resentment. Nevertheless, Dominicans readily conceded that the company was less miserly with its employees than were many domestically owned firms and that, in fact, it treated its cane cutters far better than the government did the unfortunate Haitian contractees. Furthermore, the company sponsored a social development program, providing housing, clinics, and schools for its workers, and it was generally believed that the company's international president, Charles Bluhdorn, and his family had taken a special interest in the country. At any rate, to Dominican nationalists Gulf and Western was at least a known adversary. Therefore, the news that Gulf and Western was selling off its Dominican properties was generally received with disquiet rather than relief.

After Bluhdorn's death in early 1983, Gulf and Western's new president, Martin S. Davis, decided that the company would concentrate on high-return consumer products, leisure businesses, and financial services and would divest itself of several major lines of business. The decision to sell the Dominican properties was announced in June 1984. It was said to be based on the discouraging long-term prospects for sugar exports, as well as on a decision taken the previous month by the Dominican government; the government, desperately low on foreign-exchange reserves, required exporters to turn in their dollars for local currency at an artificially low rate of exchange.[24]

It was announced in October 1984 that a purchase agreement had been reached between Gulf and Western and the Fanjul family of Florida. The transfer of ownership was completed in early January 1985. The group of investors, who acquired Gulf and Western properties in Florida as well as in the Dominican Republic, is headed by the Fanjul brothers, Alfonso and José ("Pepe"), Cuban Americans whose family had been producing sugar in Florida through the Osceola Farms Company. Other investors in the Fanjul group include the Flo-Sun Land Corporation and other Florida-based agribusiness firms and a Dominican group that had been involved in local management of Gulf

---

23. Pamela G. Hollie, "Gulf and Western to Sell Dominican Holdings," *New York Times*, June 13, 1984, pp. 1, 39.
24. *Ibid.*; and James M. Hawley III, economic counselor, U.S. Embassy, interview with the author, Santo Domingo, January 9, 1985.

and Western properties, including Carlos A. Morales Troncoso, president of the Americas Corporation.[25]

Morales Troncoso is to retain the titular presidency of the umbrella corporation, and the new owners have announced no major changes in the management of the former Gulf and Western properties. Nevertheless, the transaction has left officials of the PRD government and other Dominican political leaders uneasy. They fear that the Gulf and Western pullout might discourage other potential investors and that the anti-Castro militance of the Fanjuls and their associates might result in activities and decisions based on political rather than business criteria. Former President Bosch has even publicly suggested that La Romana might be used as a staging area for operations against Cuba.

Of course, Gulf and Western and now its successors in the Fanjul group have been only the largest sources of anxiety. The behavior of other foreign corporations and subsidiaries has been equally unaccountable and, in some cases, arrogant. Falconbridge, the country's second-largest foreign investor, has been engaged since the mid 1970s in a dispute with the government over taxes and has periodically threatened to close its nickel mine if the government presses its claims. In the 1970s, according to an SEC report, Philip Morris made an illicit $16,000 payment to a Dominican tax official; made payments amounting to $120,000 to various Dominican legislators for passage of an advantageous law; and made monthly payments of $1000 to Balaguer himself.[26]

The corruptive influences exercised by foreign companies represent only one of the detrimental aspects of the republic's circumstance of economic dependence. Dominican prosperity has been contingent from year to year on the size of its sugar quota in the U.S. market and on other import quotas and fees based on considerations of U.S. domestic and foreign policy with little regard for Dominican needs. Uncertainty about the U.S. market, coupled with the wildly fluctuating price of sugar, has rendered economic planning and forecasting almost futile.

While prices and markets for Dominican products have been uncertain, there has been a devastating certainty in the steady climb of the costs of imports essential to industrialization—imports of capital

---

25. "Gulf Termina Pasos Venta Sus Intereses Azucareros," *El Caribe*, Santo Domingo, January 10, 1985, p. 1.
26. Chomsky and Herman, *Washington Connection*, p. 246.

equipment as well as of raw materials for the production processes. This has led to increasingly serious balance-of-payments problems. The current account has not had a surplus since about 1967, and the trade deficit in the early 1980s was hovering around $100 million.[27]

The cost of imports is hardly offset by tax revenues from foreign holdings and the profits of foreign enterprises. In order to maintain a competitive advantage in attracting foreign capital, Dominican governments have felt obliged to offer generous tax holidays, high ceilings on profit repatriation, and other incentives and subsidies.[28] It must also invest its own scarce revenues in infrastructure projects beneficial to investors. The revenue gap can be bridged only by borrowing, even in times of soaring interest rates. (By 1985, the foreign debt had climbed to almost $3 billion.) Thus the price of development, or modernization, for an economy so heavily dependent on foreign markets and suppliers, foreign investors and foreign creditors is chronic insolvency. Such insolvency means, of course, that the needs of the general population for social services and welfare will not be met.

Dependent development also means, as we have seen, the decline of traditional activities, such as subsistence farming; the absorption or displacement of domestic enterprises; and the inhibition of domestic entrepreneurship. It means production for a limited domestic market and capital-intensive industrial processes that do little to alleviate unemployment. Unemployment and low wages inhibit the development of a domestic market, thus maintaining the model of production only for export and for the affluent few. Finally, over time, it means the suppression of national culture and the transplantation, in its place, of an alien culture and way of life.

A Tale of Deprivation and of Hope[29]

Before 1953, Rivera de Payabo, in the central part of the Dominican Republic, was a village of farming families. Most owned their own

27. Ruben Berrios Martínez, "Dependent Capitalism and the Prospects for Democracy in Puerto Rico and the Dominican Republic," in Paget Henry and Carl Stone (eds.), *The Newer Caribbean: Decolonization, Democracy and Development* (Philadelphia: Institute for the Study of Human Issues, 1983), pp. 327–339.
28. Companies that set up manufacturing operations in the free zones, for example, benefit from government subsidies and at the same time are 100 percent exempt from Dominican income taxes and duties.
29. Stephen Vetter, "Portrait of a Peasant Leader: Ramón Aybar," *Grassroots Development*, Vol. 8, No. 1, 1984, pp. 2–11.

4. SOCIAL AND ECONOMIC STRUCTURES

small plots of land. They had colorfully painted houses of mud and thatch, vegetable gardens, corn fields, fruit trees, and animals—chickens, pigs, and mules; some even had cattle. There were wild boars to hunt and plenty of fish in the rivers.

But Trujillo coveted their land. In 1953 he seized it to expand his already extensive sugar estates. The houses and fields were burned and bulldozed. The area was designated one large plantation, where no crops other than sugarcane—not even a family garden—could be planted without the management's permission. Some villagers migrated to the capital. Those who stayed to cut cane for the estate were crowded into grim wooden barracks called *bateyes*. The villagers lost more than their homes and crops and animals; they lost the sounds and smells and vistas of unspoiled forest. And they lost their folklore and customs of cooperation: their way of life. After Trujillo's demise, the estate was taken over and managed by the government, but little else changed.

The revitalization of Rivera de Payabo owes much to the vision and energy of one man, Ramón Aybar, a schoolteacher and poet. Aybar had continued to write about the vibrant farming community he remembered from his childhood and to believe that, amid the despoliation wrought in the name of "white gold," some of the advantages and amenities of that happier time could be re-created. One day in the mid 1970s he called a meeting of his neighbors at the local school. From that seed grew the Federation of Associations of Neighbors of Rivera de Payabo.

From the beginnings of community organization, Aybar sought to build a "perpetual motion machine." He believed that each successful project could serve as the launching pad for another. But lacking public assistance, credit, and training, the neighbors initially set limited goals. Their first project was a funeral society, as they felt that dignity began with being able to afford a proper burial. Its operation was simple: Members made regular contributions over time and from the pooled funds received a lump sum when there was a death in the family.

Apart from the funeral society, social solidarity was maintained through the revival of the tradition of *convite*—the pooling of voluntary labor—to build community centers and to pursue other common goals. With the momentum thus gathered, the association took on a more ambitious project. Rice was being cultivated in the patches of swampland scattered around the estate, but members had not been able to get a reasonable return on their excess production. The federation sought to offer members mill and warehouse services for low fees, which would then go into a marketing fund.

Seed money for the project was not available from banks, but the federation was able to obtain a grant of $44,000 in 1980 from the Inter-American Foundation, a U.S. government development agency, with which it purchased a rice mill, a small truck, and materials to construct a warehouse and seven cement drying areas for the rice. The marketing plan was frustrated by a government monopoly on the marketing of rice. (The underfunded marketing board often paid with promissory notes rather than cash.) After a run-in with authorities when the federation tried to do its own marketing, that aspect of the project was dropped. Nevertheless, the milling and storage project generated enough cash for the federation to launch another project.

With the federation's own funds plus member contributions, the federation bought eight sows and one boar. A pigpen was built, with voluntary labor, behind the mill, so that the animals could feed on the rice hulls. When the sows birthed, females from those litters were distributed to members, who returned two sows from their first litters to the federation. Their offspring were in turn distributed to other members. The federation retained and fattened the boars for sale to help underwrite the project. Each participating member ultimately had from 5 to 12 pigs.

With the returns from the rice and pig projects, the federation was able to establish a savings and loan program. It also set up a small store to offer basic agricultural commodities.

In addition to its income-generating projects, the federation sought to protect the neighbors and their environment from the consequences of the callous disregard of the estate managers. In the mid 1960s, crop dusters began to spray herbicides over the cane fields. Much of the water was poisoned. Subsistence gardens and rice plots were ruined. Workers in the fields were doused along with the cane. Several died and many others were sickened.

Aybar had sought to put a stop to the spraying in the 1960s by denouncing it through his poetry on a church-run radio station, but to no avail. After the federation was organized, Aybar met separately with the authorities to discuss the crop dusting. The authorities would agree to reconsider, but each time a new administrator took over, the spraying would begin again. Finally, federation members took matters into their own hands. They got advance notice of the spraying schedule and gathered on the runway, armed with machetes, to block the planes.

4. SOCIAL AND ECONOMIC STRUCTURES

Finally forced to deal with the concerns of the federation, the estate managers banned the more dangerous chemicals and cut down on the frequency of spraying. Though the victory was only partial, this united defense of their interests was a great source of pride to the neighbors of Rivera de Payabo. By 1984, the federation had grown to embrace 10 community associations, a youth group, and a mothers' club.

5
POLITICAL INSTITUTIONS

The Structure of Government

The republic's constitution of 1966 is the twenty-fifth to be promulgated since the expulsion of the Haitians in 1844. Like all previous Dominican constitutions, it guarantees full respect for civil liberties and human rights, although those guarantees proved ineffective during the dozen years of Balaguer's rule. The 1966 constitution built upon previous ones, particularly the constitution of 1963, although several of the 1963 document's nationalistic and social welfare features were discarded.

The Executive

The president and vice-president assume office by direct election. The president, in turn, appoints a cabinet consisting of approximately 15 officers, or "secretaries." Congressional confirmation is not required. The constitutional powers of the presidency are extensive, in part because the president must oversee the many major enterprises the state confiscated from the Trujillo family and in part because all government jobs, excepting those in the diplomatic service, are filled through patronage. There is no permanent, legally protected civil service.

Several constitutional provisions regarding the presidency were clearly intended to prevent a recurrence of military intervention under a cloak of legitimacy. The president, who serves a 4-year term, must not have been on active duty with the armed forces or the police during the year before his election. Resignation of the president or vice-president is to be accepted only if it occurs before an ad hoc session of the National Assembly. In the event of the president's death or resignation, his term is served out by the vice-president. In the event of death or resignation of a vice-president who has succeeded to the presidency, the president of the Supreme Court rules pending new presidential elections.

Guzmán would have been the first president in Dominican history to be duly elected, to complete his term without attempting to extend it, and to turn over his office to a duly elected successor. But in July 1982, 2 months after the elections, he committed suicide. Vice-President Jacobo Majluta served until the new president-elect, Salvador Jorge Blanco of the PRD, was inaugurated in August.

The constitution of 1966, like previous ones, empowers the Congress to declare a state of siege or national emergency, suspending personal liberties and allowing the president to take the actions necessary to defend the nation. If the legislature is not in session, the president may declare a state of siege or emergency on his own initiative. Balaguer rarely found it necessary to use such reserve powers because neither the legislature nor the judiciary saw fit seriously to challenge his arbitrary use of presidential powers.

A measure of the president's power can be seen in the fact that about half of all jobs in the country are ultimately controlled by him. Balaguer's austerity law, passed during his first presidential term, reduced the salaries of government employees and froze them. They remained frozen, in the face of severe inflation, through Balaguer's two additional terms. By 1977 the real incomes of undersecretaries had dropped to less than half of what they had been in 1970. The upshot was that corruption, which had long been a problem in the public service, became systematic at every level from the cabinet down. The attraction of a government job was said to depend on the size of the bribes one could extract.[1]

The extensive powers of the presidency are matched by extensive responsibilities, both constitutional and traditional. Individual citizens can and do petition the president with respect to all manner of personal and community problems. In early 1985, President Jorge Blanco, while trying to deal with a congressional boycott, a budget crisis, and IMF demands, was called upon to resolve a dispute

1. Ian Bell, *The Dominican Republic* (Boulder, CO: Westview Press, 1981).

among drivers and riders over bus routes in Santo Domingo and the interior.[2]

The president's extensive power of patronage is also a mixed blessing. PRD governments since 1978 have used the public payroll as a major means of consolidating their constituencies and combating unemployment. In 1985, however, the government was under fierce pressure from the IMF to limit public spending, and the Congress was balking on the prospect of new taxes. Nevertheless, the president, for reasons of politics (and perhaps of compassion), did not dare to pare the bloated bureaucracy.

The Legislature

The legislature, or Congress, is bicameral, consisting of the Senate and the Chamber of Deputies. Members of both chambers are elected directly for 4-year terms, coinciding with presidential terms. The Senate has 27 members, one for each province and another for the National District, Santo Domingo, elected by simple plurality. The 120 deputies are elected by a system of proportional representation from multimember districts coincident with the provinces; they are elected on the basis of 1 deputy for every 50,000 inhabitants (or fraction of more than half that number), provided that each province has at least 2 deputies.

In both houses, a quorum is half of the total membership. Normally decisions are taken by a simple majority. Most categories of legislation may be introduced by members of either house or by the president. Money bills, however, may be introduced only by the president and may be amended only by a two-thirds majority in both houses. A bill introduced and passed in one house must subsequently be passed by the other and, if amended by the second house, must be returned for reconsideration by the first. Finally, to be promulgated as law, the bill must be signed by the president. A presidential veto may be overridden by a vote of two-thirds in both houses.

The Congress meets twice annually for 90-day sessions, beginning on February 27 and on August 16. Extraordinary meetings may be convoked by the president. When the two houses meet jointly for

2. Miguel A. Matos, "Harían que Vehículos Cumplan Extensión de Rutas Asiquadas," *El Caríbe*, January 10, 1985, p. 1.

extraordinary or ceremonial sessions, the body is known as the National Assembly.

The Senate has exclusive jurisdiction in the selection of justices for the Supreme Court and judges for all lower courts; the selection of the president and members and alternates of the Central Electoral Board; the selection of members of the Accounting Commission, an agency that oversees the republic's general and special accounts; and the confirmation of diplomatic appointments submitted by the president.

Impeachment proceedings are to be initiated in the Chamber of Deputies, where a motion of impeachment requires a three-fourths majority to pass. Should such a motion pass, an impeachment trial would be conducted by the Senate.

As most opposition parties boycotted the elections of 1970 and 1974, Balaguer was never subject to restraint or challenge imposed by the legislature. His party, the PR, maintained an overwhelming majority. After the election of 1978, Guzmán's PRD had 48 deputies, and Balaguer's PR had 43. In the Senate, however, the electoral commission, still controlled by Balaguer, had ensured that the PR retain control; it had 16 seats to the PRD's 11. In the elections of 1982, the PRD took 62 seats in the lower house, the PR 47, and Bosch's Dominican Liberation party (PLD) 9; independent candidates took the 2 remaining seats. The PRD won 17 of the Senate seats, conceding the remainder to the PR.[3]

The PRD finally had a majority in the Senate. Still, the president's proposals were not necessarily well received by that body. The PRD contingent there was under the control of Majluta, who was a bitter rival of Jorge Blanco within the party.

The Judiciary

The country's legal system, unlike those of most Latin American countries, is based on the Napoleonic Code. The French model had been imposed by the Haitian occupation force. When the Haitians withdrew in 1844, the Napoleonic Code was retained, although 40 years were to pass before the Code was officially translated into Spanish.

3. Rolando Alum, Jr., "Dominican Republic," in George E. Delury (ed.), *World Encyclopedia of Political Systems and Parties*, Vol. 1 (New York: Facts on File, 1983), p. 267.

All judges are required to have law degrees; the number of years in legal practice required for qualification varies in accordance with the level in the judicial hierarchy. Justices of the Supreme Court must have a track record of 12 years in legal practice.

The Supreme Court, at the apex of the judicial system, has nine members, one of whom is designated by the Senate to serve as chairman. It is the ultimate court of appeal and has original jurisdiction in cases involving the president, vice-president, members of the cabinet and of Congress, and judges and prosecutors of the higher courts. The Court also has administrative functions embracing the whole of the judicial system, including the suspension or dismissal and transfer of judges of lower courts.

Lower courts include 7 courts of appeal; 15 land courts, on the same hierarchical level as the courts of appeal, which deal exclusively with disputes involving real property; 27 courts of first instance; and a continually expanding number of justice of the peace courts—in principal, at least one for each municipality. There are also a number of special courts, created by law rather than by the constitution. These include juvenile, labor, electoral, and military tribunals.

The Dominican judiciary cannot be said to be independent, as the vital safeguard of irremovability of judges is missing. Judges serve 4-year renewable terms coincident with the terms of elected officials. Thus, those who wish to remain on the bench must take into consideration the political climate and the tilt of official policy when interpreting the law and rendering judgment.[4]

Provincial and Local Government

Each of the country's 26 provinces is headed by a governor appointed by the president. There are no provincial legislatures, and provincial governments have little independence from the central government. President Balaguer, beginning in his first term, took the unprecedented step of appointing only women to the provincial governorship—this on the claim that women were less readily corrupted. Subsequent PRD governments have not followed that precedent. Most of their appointees have been men.

The provinces are subdivided into 96 municipalities *(municipios)*, equivalent to townships or counties, embracing a central town and its

---

4. Bell, *Dominican Republic*, pp. 204–205.

outlying villages. Municipal mayors and councillors are elected by direct vote every 4 years. The size of a municipal council depends on the population it represents, but it must have at least five members. Municipal governments provide water and sewage works, fire protection, street maintenance, garbage collection, and other such services. They may levy taxes provided that those taxes do not conflict with national legislation.

The National District, with about 20 percent of the national population, is governed as a municipality. Its mayoralty is a position of considerable prominence in the national system. In 1982 the secretary-general of the PRD, José Francisco Peña Gómez, was elected to that position. Balaguer's party, however, has continued to control a substantial majority of the smaller municipalities.

The Electoral System

The electoral system, established with the technical assistance of the OAS prior to the elections of 1962, was incorporated in broad outline into the constitution of 1966. It includes a hierarchy of electoral boards presided over by the Central Election Board (JCE), whose members are chosen by the Senate. Members of the Central Board serve 12-year terms. Provincial and municipal board members are selected by and serve at the pleasure of the Central Board.

The franchise extends to all citizens 18 years of age or older and to younger citizens who are married. In the early 1980s it was estimated that at least 90 percent of eligible voters were registered; about 85 percent of those registered turned out to vote in 1978, and almost 90 percent turned out in 1982. Voting was compulsory, though that provision was not enforced. Election days are legal holidays, on which the selling of liquor is prohibited. Apart from the military and police contingents assigned to guard polling places and ballots, military personnel are confined to barracks. Members of the police and the armed forces on active duty are prohibited from voting.

National and local offices are contested concurrently every 4 years in the month of May. Polls are open from 6:00 a.m. to 6:00 p.m. Ballots are color coded and bear party emblems because of the high level of illiteracy—over 30 percent—of adult Dominicans. Voters receive two ballots for each party running candidates, and deposit one for the presidential election and another for all other contested offices. Such a system effectively discourages ticket splitting. It also lends itself to a simple form of coercion. Before the 1978 elections, for example, some public employees were told not to show up for work if they could not turn back their unused white PRD ballots to their supervisors.[5]

The Contemporary Party System

The Dominican party system remains a multiparty one. Twenty parties, most of them tiny, were registered just before the elections of 1982, but only 14 of those participated in the elections. Of those that participated, only 5 retained legal status after the elections. Six others retained legal status by refraining from participation, but some of them have since dissolved or merged with other parties. The registration of a new party is a relatively simple matter, but the party must win at least 5 percent of the popular vote or obtain congressional representation to retain its legal status.[6]

All parties of significant size and durability draw, to some extent, from the same social bases. All look to the social and economic elites for some degree of financial support, to upper and middle classes for leadership, and to the poor masses for votes. The two major parties have dues-paying members throughout the country and contest local as well as national offices. Campaigning has become increasingly professionalized, sophisticated, and expensive, making use of trained pollsters, fund raisers, and media consultants.

The results, on paper, of the elections of 1978 and 1982 made it appear that the system was moving sharply toward two-party dominance. The presidential candidates of the two major parties drew about 94 percent of the vote in 1978 and about 84 percent in 1982. In fact, it is more likely that the system faces a convulsion of fragmentation and realignment before the end of the decade and that there will be room in the new configuration for at least three sizable parties or coalitions.

The Dominican Revolutionary Party (PRD)

The PRD presents itself as a party of the center−left; it is social democratic in the European mold and a member of the Socialist International. The party takes pride in having institutionalized civilian

---

5. Adrian Rodriguez and Deborah Huntington, "Dominican Republic—the Launching of a Democracy," *NACLA Report on the Americas*, Vol. 16, No. 6, November−December 1982, p. 5.
6. Julio Brea Franco, *El sistema constitucional dominicano*, Vol. 2 (Santo Domingo: Universidad Nacional Pedro Henríquez Ureña, 1983), pp. 686−727.

democratic government in the republic. It still seeks a deepening of the process of economic development—a more equitable distribution of goods and services and of income and opportunity—although it has been moderated by age and experience. Its economic nationalism has been tempered considerably since the 1960s; its leaders now welcome foreign investment, but only as long, they say, as investors are willing to live within the confines of Dominican law.[7]

The party's opponents, on both the right and left, allege that it has become just another party of "the establishment." In fact, as is generally the case when a reformist party comes to power, its ideological profile has been blurred. Differences within the party—from socialists to opportunists to feudalists—are almost as great as within the society as a whole.

The PRD is well organized. It claims some 10,000 grass-roots committees *(comités de base)* with a minimum membership of 32 and a maximum of 64. Thus its overall membership might approach half a million, and that does not take into account the affiliated organizations of women, youth, and various categories of workers and professionals.[8]

The party is strongest in the cities, among workers and professionals, but it draws support from all social classes and from all parts of the country. It is also reasonably well financed, in part from dues, but also, reportedly, from contributions from European social democratic parties. To a greater extent than its major rivals, the PRD follows democratic procedures in its internal affairs, such as the selection of delegates to national conventions and the nomination of candidates for public office. Grass-roots committees elect delegates to municipal bodies, which in turn elect delegates to regional and national conventions.

José Francisco Peña Gómez has been the driving force behind the PRD at least since Bosch left the party in 1973 and, for all but symbolic purposes, since Bosch's government was toppled in 1963. The party's leadership has been collegiate, at least in form, because Peña Gómez has encouraged the rise of other leaders.[9] He has promoted Guzmán, Majluta, and Jorge Blanco in turn and has tried to maintain balance

---

7. Vicente Sánchez, president of the PRD, interview with the author.
8. Winston Arnaud, acting secretary-general of the PRD, interview with the author, January 10, 1985.
9. Sánchez and Arnaud, interviews.

among competing factions by favoring one faction, for example, for the presidency and another for congressional leadership. This has often resulted in intraparty stalemate, but for more than 10 years—since the defection of Bosch and his loyalists—it has prevented major schisms.

Guzmán, a wealthy rancher from the party's right wing, was promoted not because of his strength within the party but because of his acceptability outside of it—in particular, with the oligarchy and the United States. As president, he was consistently at odds with other party leaders. Locked in bitter rivalry with Jorge Blanco, Guzmán attempted to label him a leftist. Jorge Blanco was a leftist, however, only in relation to Guzmán. Blanco's "credentials" on the left derived primarily from his representation, as a prominent attorney, of alleged leftists detained by the Balaguer government. But his clients had also included wealthy ranchers and businessmen.

Since Guzmán's suicide, the party has more or less settled into three factions, headed, respectively, by Jorge Blanco, Majluta, and Peña Gómez. Majluta, having inherited the following of Guzmán, has become the standard-bearer of the party's right wing. Virtually since the beginning of Jorge Blanco's term, Majluta has been campaigning for the PRD nomination for the presidency in 1986. He has even established a parallel pseudo party, known as *La Estructura* (The Structure), to promote his candidacy at home and among Dominican emigrants in Puerto Rico and on the U.S. mainland. He has a considerable following among middle-level party functionaries, but among PRD leaders only Peña Gómez has an identifiable and mobilizable popular base.

Jorge Blanco's faction consists largely of technocrats. He has no strong base of his own either among party activists or among the masses. His popular base was, in effect, loaned to him by Peña Gómez. Jorge Blanco has had his differences with Peña Gómez, but would probably support him for the presidency in 1986 in order to block Majluta. Without a dramatic turnabout in the economy before 1986, however, the support of Jorge Blanco would be, at best, a mixed blessing.[10]

Peña Gómez, a powerful orator, is the party's most charismatic figure, having a large personal following among the poor of Santo Domingo. He has long been the party's official secretary-general, but

---

10. Ramón Martínez-Portorreal, lawyer, law professor, and executive secretary of the Dominican Committee on Human Rights, interviews with the author, Santo Domingo, November 26, 1982, and January 7, 1985.

has temporarily turned over the responsibilities of that position to Winston Arnaud while Peña Gómez serves as mayor of Santo Domingo. Peña Gómez's offices at City Hall are always aswarm with visitors and petitioners—from European newsmen to community leaders to individuals seeking personal assistance.[11]

Peña Gómez's presidential prospects have been clouded by the fact that he is black—the son of Haitian victims of the massacre of 1937—and lacking in personal wealth. His Haitian antecedents, plus the fact that he has a popular base in the urban poor, have contributed to making him the bête noir of the Dominican armed forces. (Military officers often refer to him as the "Haitian communist.")[12] While serving as the spokesman of the urban poor, he has often found himself, under PRD governments, in the unenviable position of being called on to restrain his followers. He has, in fact, served as a moderating influence on his followers and in general on the party's left wing, and his rhetoric, of late, has been muted. Nevertheless, there remains some doubt as to whether the Dominican armed forces and their U.S. patrons would allow him to assume the presidency.

There is also some doubt as to whether Majluta and his followers would stay with the PRD if Peña Gómez emerges as its presidential candidate. The schism between Majluta and other PRD leaders is profound, and some Dominicans predict that both the PRSC and the PRD will be subject to fragmentation and realignment in the late 1980s. Majluta's faction might then merge with one of the factions of the PRSC.[13]

The Reformist Social Christian Party (PRSC)

The new PRSC, established in mid 1984, represents a merger of the Reformist party (PR) and the Revolutionary Social Christian party (PRSC). For the PR, the merger, long sought by Balaguer, means access to the diplomatic and financial support of the international Christian Democratic movement. For the Social Christians, it means votes and

---

11. On the day I visited, one of the petitioners, an elderly woman, asked him for 1000 pesos for a funeral; he gave her 500.
12. Richard Hines, political counselor, U.S. Embassy, interview with the author, Santo Domingo, January 3, 1985.
13. Guido D'Alessandro, businessman; founding member of Social Christian party; former ambassador, cabinet member, and member of the congress; interviews with the author, Boca Chica and Santo Domingo, January 4, 11, and 13, 1985.

the prospect of a new political base. It is a marriage, like most, in which a certain amount of competition is to be expected, but in which the conveniences are presumed to outweigh the inconveniences.

The PR has generally been described as a party of the center–right, since it has represented the interests of big business, foreign and domestic. Nevertheless, many of its members have had little more in common than personal loyalty to Balaguer and, between 1966 and 1978, an appreciation of the advantages of belonging to the official party. The party has also been described as *caudillista*, or populist, as its popular support has derived from Balaguer's personal standing among the rural poor. Its lack of a clear programmatic or ideological base has sometimes appeared to be a strategic advantage in a country with little experience in open political competition.

Organizationally, the PR fell heir to much of the political infrastructure, especially in rural areas, of the Trujillo era. That infrastructure was provided largely by the armed forces. Observers friendly to the PR claim that the rural vote was delivered by the military because the soldiers came from the rural areas, and each of them influenced the vote of his extended family. Other observers maintain that, at least while Balaguer was in power, the military delivered the rural vote for the PR through coercion and intimidation. Nevertheless, it is clear that in much of the countryside Balaguer is genuinely popular.

In the opposition since 1978, the PR has maintained much of its support among the rural poor and has made inroads into the cities as well. Urban support has come from first-generation migrants from the countryside and, increasingly, from the middle class. Traditionally antioligarchic, the PR had reached out also to embrace old enemies from the oligarchy. Donald Reid Cabral, for example, had become the party's director of organization.

The party's strong showing in public opinion polls in the mid 1980s owed much to the misfortunes and failures of the PRD. Although the land distribution carried out by Balaguer was very limited in relation to the need and to the aspirations of the short-lived Bosch government, it was impressive compared to the performance of PRD governments since 1978. Looking back through rose-colored glasses, many remembered the extensive public works and the lower prices of the Balaguer years and thus misremembered those years as a time of general rather than selective prosperity.

Party organization is democratic in structure, as local party organizations are supposed to elect delegates to the national conference. In practice, however, democratic procedures have not necessarily been followed; the party has been overwhelmingly dominated by Balaguer. Like the PRD, it collects dues from its members, although party activities were largely funded from government resources while Balaguer was in power. Joaquín Ricardo, Balaguer's "nephew" (actually second cousin), who serves as secretary-general of the new PRSC, concedes that the party is not as well organized as the PRD. He estimates that it has some 50,000 local leaders and a few hundred thousand members, but most who vote PR do not register with the party.[14]

Balaguer, now in his 70s, in poor health and nearly blind, is gearing up for another campaign for the presidency—with reasonable prospects for success. But he has no heir apparent in the party; until very recently he had discouraged the development of other leaders. He may now be grooming his nephew to replace him. Ricardo, educated in political science in the United States, appears to relish the political game, but he is young and inexperienced.

Another likely contender for the mantle of leadership is Fernando Alvarez Boegart. In 1978, when the party, through democratic procedures, nominated him as its vice-presidential candidate, Balaguer vetoed that choice and selected his own running mate. In 1982, however, Alvarez again won the party's nomination for vice-president, and on that occasion Balaguer was unable to unseat him.

In fact, with Balaguer's death or incapacitation, competition for leadership of the party will doubtless be fierce, and there is some fear among the party's leaders and supporters that it will simply disintegrate. Ricardo believes that the merger with the Social Christians will prove crucial to the survival of the PR.

The Social Christians bring to the new party precisely what the Reformistas lacked: solid ideological grounding, well-developed programs, and well-trained and experienced leaders. What the Social Christians lacked was a political space in the Dominican party system.

The original PRSC, after a promising beginning in the 1960s, declined in the 1970s, placing a poor fourth in the elections of 1978. In the 1960s, the party's greatest influence on national politics derived from its ties with the Autonomous Confederation of Christian Unions (CASC), but the union has since distanced itself from the party. Although the PRSC aligned itself with the PRD in the 1960s, some of its leaders accepted government positions during Balaguer's long rule. In

---

14. Joaquín Ricardo, interview with the author, Santo Domingo, January 11, 1985.

1982, a portion of the party supported Balaguer for the presidency, but two factions had spun off to form other minor parties.

The Social Christians have not become as conservative as the Reformistas. They still seek means of avoiding or mitigating the excesses of both capitalism and Marxist–Leninism. Guido D'Alessandro, one of the founders of the original PRSC, told me that the Social Christians have not moved to the right socially and economically, only politically. When they were young, they had no alternative to seeking their political goals by revolutionary means—to demonstrating on the streets and meeting underground. Now they can afford to be more practical. As they see it, the rural masses who have been loyal to the PR have no ideology. If the Social Christians can begin to organize and educate the rural poor, they may be able to occupy that political space and build a base for their party after Balaguer passes from the scene.[15]

The Dominican Liberation Party (PLD)

On the basis of its standing in the elections of 1978, or even of its vastly improved standing in the elections of 1982, Juan Bosch's PLD might be characterized as a minor party. But its star has continued to rise, and in the mid 1980s leaders of the major parties were beginning to take the PLD challenge seriously.

The party received only about 18,000 votes in the elections of 1978, causing to to lose legal status. But it went through the petitioning process again in order to register for the 1982 elections. At that time, it won nearly 10 percent of the vote, placing third after the PRD and the PR. A public opinion poll released in 1984 gave the PLD an approval rating of about 25 percent, trailing the PRSC but running ahead of the ruling PRD.[16] Seasoned observers did not consider the poll to be highly scientific; nor did they assume that the fickle electorate would maintain the views reflected in it until the next elections in 1986. Nevertheless, it was clear to all that the PRD was in political trouble and that the PLD was consequently attracting new support.

The PLD remains a personalist party, firmly dominated by its founder—a matter that has generated discontent and schisms. The party's public information officer maintains that no one except Bosch

---

15. D'Alessandro, interview.
16. Frank Moya Pons, "La Política Dominicana: Agosto 1984," *LASA Forum*, Vol. 15, No. 3, Fall 1984, pp. 19–21.

can speak for—or even about—the party.[17] Even technical information, such as the size of the party's membership, is withheld unless Bosch himself chooses to release it. The PLD suffered some setbacks in 1984, as a new coalition on the far left displaced it from its dominant position in the General Confederation of Labor (CGT) and at the Autonomous University of Santo Domingo (UASD). Nevertheless, it is clear that the party has drawn enormous crowds for recent rallies and demonstrations. Its weekly newspaper, *Vanguardia del Pueblo*, has a circulation of about 50,000.

Bosch is anything but enigmatic; he continues to pronounce at great length on the state of the nation and the world. Yet there is little agreement among the politically articulate as to his current stance and motives. His old enemies on the far right continue to call him a communist. Leaders of the Dominican Communist party (PCD) say that is nonsense, that he is a reformist, not a revolutionary. In fact, his concerns seem to have changed little in the course of his political career. He remains, above all, irreverent. He still lambasts the "imperialistic" designs of the United States and the IMF and the greed of foreign investors, and deplores high prices, low wages, and the inadequacy of social services. What has changed is that his erstwhile colleagues of the PRD are now in power, and his harshest criticisms are directed toward the corruption he sees as rampant in the PRD government.

Several political leaders who have known Bosch for decades—as ally or adversary or both—believe that he does not want to win the presidency again, given the straitjacket that, at least for the foreseeable future, any Dominican president will wear. They believe that, concerned about his place in history, he thinks that only in the opposition can he maintain his integrity.[18]

At any rate, it is most unlikely that either the United States or the Dominican military would allow Bosch to assume the presidency again. Bosch's followers in the PLD may well increase their representation in Congress, but Bosch himself, like his old rival Balaguer, is in his 70s, and no prospective future leader for the PLD has emerged.

As to Bosch's place in history, assessments of his political role will no

---

17. Euclides Gutiérrez Félix, Public Information Office, Partido de Liberacion Dominicana (PLD).
18. One of the several Dominican leaders who expressed this opinion was Moreno Martínez.

doubt be mixed. His place as a scholar, however, is already assured. Even his bitterest rivals cite his analyses of Dominican politics and society.

Minor Parties

Minor parties on the left were emasculated by assassination and deportation after the abortive revolution of 1965, and some of the leaders of minor right-of-center parties that had functioned in the early 1960s were absorbed by the PR. Groups identifying themselves as parties continued to appear and vanish in revolving-door fashion, but they generally represented the atomization of older parties rather than the mobilization of new groups.

General Wessín, using the vestige of this PQD, contested the presidency in the elections of 1982; but he gained only 1.3 percent of the vote, and the party lost its legal status. A later generation of cashiered generals, assembled in the Partido Nacional de Veteranos Civiles (National party of Retired Veterans), supported the candidacy of Balaguer, as did remnants of the UCN and the MIDA and the tiny Partido de Acción Nacional.

Several minuscule parties united in coalition or spun off from larger parties to enter the elections of 1982. The Alianza Social Demócrata (ASD), a splinter of the PRD, supported the presidential candidacy of José Rafael Abinader, who had served in the cabinet of President Guzmán. He won only some 9000 votes, but in early 1985 was already campaigning for the election of 1986.

On the left, the Movimiento por el Socialismo (MPS) joined the Dominican Communist party (PCD) in the Unidad Socialista in support of the candidacy of PCD leader Narciso Isa Conde, while the Bloque Socialista (BS) and the Union Patriotica (UPA), themselves coalitions of smaller parties, formed the Izquierda Unida to back journalist Rafael Francisco ("Fafa") Tavares. The combined total of the two coalitions was 1.29 percent of the vote.[19]

In June of 1983, the two leftist coalitions merged to form the Frente Izquierdista Dominicana (FID), the Dominican Leftist Front. The front at one time claimed 12 individual parties, but a few have since defected. The PCD, the dominant party within the coalition, is led by young intellectuals, but seeks support among urban workers, peas-

---

19. Brea, *El sistema constitucional dominicano*.

ants, university students, and would-be workers in the shantytowns of the larger cities. Illegal and persecuted during most of its history, the party was given legal status just before the elections of 1978. It has operated freely and openly since that time, although its leaders have been subject to harassment by the police. Several of them were detained on a half-dozen occasions between the riots of April 1984 and the end of that year.[20]

The visibility and bargaining power of the left are greater than its poor performance at the voting booth would suggest. In the mid 1980s, the FID commanded the loyalty of a majority within the CGT and was the dominant political force on the campus of the UASD. It also appeared to be in the strongest position among the new committees for popular struggle (*comités de lucha popular*—CLPs) that had begun to form in poor neighborhoods in 1984 in response to dramatic increases in prices for basic foodstuffs. The PLD and PRD were competing with the FID, however, for control of those neighborhood organizations.[21]

A promising new party that has yet to be tested in elections is the Fuerza Nacional Progresista (FNP). It was organized in July 1980 and was registered prior to the election of 1982 but did not choose to enter candidates. The party, still in its formative stage, is the vehicle of Marino Vinicio ("Vincho") Castillo, a widely experienced lawyer and long-time associate of Balaguer.

As a young lawyer in San Francisco de Macorís, Castillo was drafted by Trujillo, 2 months before has assassination in 1961, to serve in the national legislative assembly. Later that year, Castillo became labor minister under Balaguer. He often spoke for Balaguer during the latter's years in exile, and in the early 1970s he drafted an agrarian-reform law for the Balaguer government. He has maintained his interest in agrarian problems and his advocacy of agrarian reform, and will seek his political base among the rural poor.[22]

The strategy of the FNP is to draw the bulk of the *reformista* vote after Balaguer becomes incapacitated. Castillo maintains that the Social Christians—intellectual, ideological, and elitist—will not be able to inherit a populist party. Others point out, however, that Castillo may

---

20. Damian Jiménez, member of the Executive Council, Partido Comunista Dominicana (PCD), interview with the author, Santo Domingo, January 10, 1985.
21. Hines, interview.
22. Vincho Castillo, interview with the author, Santo Domingo, January 4, 1985.

5. POLITICAL INSTITUTIONS

also be too theoretical and intellectual for such a party. Most observers see the FNP as right of center because of Castillo's past political alliances and his adamant anticommunism. Some, however, would place it on the left because his ideas for agrarian reform must be highly disturbing to the landowning class.

6

SOCIAL SECTORS AND INTEREST GROUPS

The Economic Elite

The individuals, families, and organizations that occupied the upper strata among landowners, businessmen, and professionals have never constituted a monolithic oligarchy, although in their opposition to Bosch in 1963 they gave the appearance of being a unified group. The Independent Democratic Action (ADI), an ad hoc group formed in 1963 by the merger of business and landowning groups, was particularly visible during that period. It directed the "Christian affirmation" movement that staged mass rallies against President Bosch just before his government was overthrown.

The so-called new rich, whose fortunes were made through the industrialization of the Trujillo era, have tended to be more adamantly opposed to reform and more alarmed by the arousal of the political consciousness of the poor than the "old" artistocratic families, whose wealth had been based on land. Many of the latter group lost both land and many of the perquisites of their social status under Trujillo, although some have gone into business and share the social and political orientations of the more numerous new rich. In general, the rich, old and new, and the associations that represent them have remained highly conservative, although no social groups have been immune to the generational dimensions of political polarization. The 1965 civil war precipitated severe crises and divisions within middle- and upper-class families and within and among professional groups.

The skewed prosperity of the late 1960s and early 1970s further enhanced the political leverage of the economic elite vis-à-vis that of other social sectors. This elite, particularly the new rich having ties with international markets, transnational corporations, or both, has become the most potent single force in Dominican politics with the possible exception of the military. This elite has not concentrated its energies on a single party; rather, it attempts to control, or at least to influence strongly, both major parties and several minor ones as well. Even Bosch's PLD is largely bankrolled by a member of the Dominican oligarchy. In general, the sometimes conflicting strategies of the economic elite are played out through the maintenance of balances and dependencies.

A symbiotic relationship of sorts exists between the civilian economic elite and the military, despite tensions based on race and class and on competition for the economic fruits of political leverage. The mere fact of being surrounded by so much poverty leaves the wealthy feeling insecure and in need of the protection only a loyal military establishment can provide. Nevertheless, the burgeoning tourist trade gives the elite an increasing stake in the maintenance of civilian government and may discourage its members from knocking on the barracks doors in times of distress.[1]

The private sector, as such, is represented by an immensely powerful umbrella organization, the National Businessmen's Council (Consejo Nacional de Hombres de Empresa—CNHE). The council's 44 affiliates represent a broad range of enterprises. They include virtually all the important associations of Dominican landowners, industrialists, bankers, and merchants, as well as representatives of foreign interests. Among CNHE's affiliates are the Japanese and American chambers of commerce. The American Chamber alone represents more than 500 U.S. and Dominican businesses.

The new president of the CNHE, Mario Cabrera, elected in November 1984 and installed in office in January 1985, is an engineer and former president of the Dominican Association of Industries. The 10 members of the executive council elected and installed at the same time represent a variety of economic interests. The organization's Commission on Economic Affairs was engaged in a "dialogue" with the Jorge Blanco government concerning means of balancing the budget and reaching a new agreement with the IMF. Not surprisingly, the council believed that the budget crisis could and must be solved without the imposition of new taxes.[2]

1. Ramón Martínez, interview with the author, Santo Domingo, January 7, 1985.
2. *El Caríbe*, January 9 and 10, 1985.

6. SOCIAL SECTORS AND INTEREST GROUPS

Organized Labor

The labor code and the constitutional provisions governing labor–management relations in the Dominican Republic have been and remain a straitjacket for Dominican workers. Public or utility employees are prohibited from striking or undertaking any sort of job action under any circumstances. That provision covers about half of the country's workers. For workers in other categories, strikes and other job actions are permissible only under certain narrowly defined circumstances in matters strictly relating to labor, rather than to politics. Unions, federations, and confederations are required to register with the Department of Labor, and such registration may be denied if an organization is found to have engaged in political activities or to have broken any labor laws. Such protections as exist—for example, minimum wages and working hours—are applicable only to private enterprises employing more than 10 workers; thus government employees and most rural workers are excluded.[3]

While labor legislation has been designed to minimize political activity, it has been *only* through political activity that labor has achieved any notable gains. Organized labor's most successful period to date was the early 1960s, when the party and the presidential candidate it had supported (Bosch and the PRD) were in office. Labor was, however, divided into three major groups. On the democratic left were the Labor Front for Union Autonomy–Labor Center for Dominican Workers (FOUPSA–CESITRADO), closely associated with the PRD, and the Autonomous Confederation of Christian Unions (CASC), affiliated with the PRSC. The National Confederation of Free Laborers (CONATRAL), organized under the auspices of the American Institute for Free Labor Development (AIFLD), emphasized collective bargaining and discouraged the pursuit of social reform through political action. The strategically important teachers and government employees unions tended to look to Castro's interpretation of Marxism. Other communist unions had been organized, but until the civil war was under way, their strength was insignificant.[4]

After Bosch's election to the presidency, with the overwhelming

---

3. Carlos Villaverde, interview with the author, Santo Domingo, January 8, 1985.
4. Howard J. Wiarda, "The Dominican Republic after the Revolution," in Richard R. Fagen and Wayne A. Cornelius, Jr. (eds.), *Political Power in Latin America: Seven Confrontations* (Englewood Cliffs, NJ: Prentice-Hall, 1970), pp. 290–294.

support of labor, the PRD initiated a movement to unit all the labor organizations into a single federation. All the major groups, with the exception of the CONATRAL, indicated an interest in formal or informal unity in support of Bosch's government. The CONATRAL, influenced by the anticommunist orientation of the U.S. government, business, and labor sponsors of the AIFLD, opposed the creation of a unified labor front and sought to diminish support for the PRD within the labor movement.

Within a few months of the election, the labor movement was sharply polarized, as FOUPSA–CESITRADO continued to call for unity in support of the Bosch government and CONATRAL denounced that government and called on the armed forces to defend the country against what it viewed as the communist menace. When Bosch was overthrown on September 25, 1963, FOUPSA–CESITRADO and CASC bitterly condemned the coup, whereas CONATRAL praised the "patriotic gesture" of the armed forces and expressed support for the Triumvirate.

Between the 1963 coup and the outbreak of civil strife in 1965 the officers of the FOUPSA–CESITRADO were periodically imprisoned, and their offices were raided by the police. In contrast, CONATRAL enjoyed a harmonious relationship with the government. The FOUPSA–CESITRADO and CASC were among the first groups to rally to the side of the Constitutionalist forces in 1965. The leadership of CONATRAL opposed the Constitutionalist revolt, but was unable to prevent its members from participating. As a consequence of its position during that struggle, CONATRAL, which had been the largest single confederation, was discredited among workers and lost control of many of its most important unions.[5]

In the 1966 elections CONATRAL supported Balaguer, while most other labor organizations supported Bosch. By the early 1970s CASC had become the strongest of the labor confederations. On the political spectrum, it was moving toward the left, while its mentor, the PRSC, moved right. The FOUPSA–CESITRADO, experiencing persecution and fragmentation during the Balaguer years, ultimately disintegrated. Some of its member unions moved left to align with the communist-dominated "La Unión" Others moved right to join a new federation called the syndicated Confederation of Organized Labor

---

5. Carlos María Gutiérrez, *The Dominican Republic: Rebellion and Repression*, trans. Richard E. Edwards (New York: Monthly Review Press, 1972), pp. 35–42.

6. SOCIAL SECTORS AND INTEREST GROUPS

(COSTO). The COSTO, in effect the successor to CONATRAL, was basically supportive of the Balaguer government.

Generally speaking, the Balaguer era was devastating to workers, whether organized or not. Average wages were lower, at least in real terms, and in some cases in monetary terms as well, by the end of the 1970s than they had been at the end of the 1960s. The labor movement had been weakened organizationally, both by repression and by schisms, although some optimists felt that this loss had been compensated to some extent by gains in political consciousness among the rank and file.

The return of the PRD to government in 1978 appeared to give organized labor a new lease on life, although the movement remained severely disadvantaged by restrictive legislation and constitutional provisions, as well as by chronically high unemployment in urban areas and the survival of near feudal patron–client relations in most rural areas. Only 12 percent of the labor force was organized in 1984. In foreign-owned agribusiness, company unions and "sweetheart" contracts were common.

Unemployment levels of 20 percent or higher have meant that workers who sought to organize their colleagues or who otherwise displeased their employers could easily be replaced. Strikes remained illegal under most circumstances; and even where strikes, legal or otherwise, have been attempted, they have generally been short-lived and unsuccessful. The unions themselves have virtually no funds to sustain their members, and strikers have no social security benefits to tide them over.

By the early 1980s, the PRD had put together a new confederation, the General Union of Dominican Workers (UGTD). Dominant among workers at La Romana, it claimed some 35,000 members and was growing fast. But it had yet to overtake the communist-dominated General Confederation of Labor (CGT), successor of "La Unión," which claimed about 40,000 members. The CGT remained strong among teachers' unions. The PLD contested FID control of the CGT in the spring of 1984. It lost, but in the process managed to spin off a dissident faction. The new organization of PLD supporters is known as the Majoritarian PGT (PGT Mayoritaria)—presumably because it is a minority faction![6] Still stronger was the CASC, with some 70,000 members. The *Cristianos*, or Christian, in its label had been changed to

---

6. Richard Hines, interview with the author, Santo Domingo, January 3, 1985.

Clasistas, in reference to its affiliation with the Christian Democratic Confederación Latinoamericano Sindical (CLAS). It was particularly strong among workers in the state-controlled sugar industry.

Peasant Movements

Participation by the peasantry in the political processes since the assassination of Trujillo has been sporadic. There were notable efforts to mobilize them in 1962 and 1963, and for a brief period the National Federation of Farmers' Brotherhoods (FENHERCA), affiliated with the PRD, had a membership of some 300,000. But after the fall of the Bosch government, peasant organizations were particularly vulnerable to reprisals by the military and the police. The FENHERCA all but disappeared as a mass organization. It reemerged as a skeletal organization in 1965 but played no significant role in the civil strife of that year, most of which took place in the capital.

By the 1980s, a number of new movements and organizations had come into being in the rural areas. The most important of these is the Independent Peasant Movement (Movimiento Campesino Independiente—MCI), organized in 1975. It has grown very fast since 1978 and by 1985 claimed some 75,000 members.

The MCI is a national organization, but is strongest in the southwest—in the areas around Barahona and Azuay, for example—where nature is stingy and the struggle for survival is particularly desperate. The movement embraces the landless as well as tenant farmers and owners of small plots. No political party has established dominance over the movement, but the PRD, PLD, and FID have all attracted adherents from its ranks.[7]

The Roman Catholic Church

The Dominican Church traditionally sought to protect its own interests through identifying with the wealthy and powerful. That pattern was maintained even through most of the awful era of Trujillo. The pastoral letter protesting the mass arrests in January 1960, however, recovered for the Church a measure of the popular esteem lost during

7. Ramón Martínez, interview.

6. SOCIAL SECTORS AND INTEREST GROUPS

the years in which it did not publicly criticize Trujillo. The political influence of Catholic leaders, which derived from the religious sentiments of the majority of the people rather than from institutional wealth or legal privilege, became considerable, particularly in rural areas.

The political emphasis of various Roman Catholic elements differed. After the end of the Trujillo period, the Vatican tried to identify the Church with democratic reforms. The peacekeeping and humanitarian efforts of the papal nuncio during the civil strife of 1965 were construed by some of the more conservative clerics and laymen as assistance to the Constitutionalist forces. Demonstrations were organized against him, and *Communist Embassy* was painted on the walls of the Nunciatura. In both 1962 and 1966 the Dominican hierarchy declined to endorse political candidates. Individual bishops, however, publicly questioned provisions of the 1963 constitution, and most were believed to be conservative. A number of individual priests, including Spanish Jesuits previously expelled from Cuba, and prominent laymen campaigned against Bosch in 1962 and subsequently worked for his ouster.

Some of the younger and more liberal clerics, inspired by the emphasis of Pope John XXIII on social and economic justice, had begun in the early 1960s to form peasant cooperatives and to work closely with labor. The PRSC and the confederation affiliated with it, with considerable support from liberal clerics, opposed the Triumvirate. They endorsed the Constitutionalist movement and favored Bosch's candidacy.

As with other sectors of the population, the civil war deepened the already existing cleavage within the Church; the generation gap, in particular, became more pronounced. Changes in the Church hierarchy after that upheaval elevated a number of the younger and more liberal clergymen. Such changes were reflected in a pastoral letter issued by the country's bishops in 1968, calling for an equitable distribution of land, and in a number of strong statements in the early 1970s on behalf of the Church condemning the government for its failure to protect human rights and to improve standards of living for the majority.

As most other national institutions that might have spoken for the dissident and the devastated had been crushed or were more vulnerable to government reprisal, the Church—or at least some elements within it—became the refuge of last resort for would-be victims of military and police repression and the only effective spokesman of those who were being victimized by regressive economic policies. Since the peak in the early 1970s of the violent repression of the Balaguer years, and particularly since the inception of democratic government in 1978, the importance of the Church in the political system has diminished.

The Church has been able to expand its pastoral functions in recent decades. Whereas until 1953 the Dominican Church was under a single archbishopric, it now has eight separate bishoprics spread throughout the country. Through its pastoral role, as well as its role as a provider of services, particularly in health and education, the Church maintains an important indirect influence on politics; the values and attitudes it imparts are surely reflected to some extent in political behavior, but there is discord within the Church hierarchy and among the faithful as to the extent of direct Church involvement in policy debate and candidate promotion that is appropriate.

Furthermore, compared to the government itself and to traditional and new economic elites the Church has very limited resources. The ratio of priests to parishioners is very low, particularly in rural areas, and the Dominican Church remains largely an alien one; Dominican nationals are badly underrepresented in the priesthood. Although more than 90 percent of the population is nominally Catholic, Protestant missions are steadily making inroads. The erosion of the Church's influence on traditional social issues is indicated by the country's very liberal divorce laws, designed to attract foreigners, and the state-supported family-planning program, both of which were introduced by Balaguer.

Divisions within the Church in the mid 1980s tended to reflect the conflicting views and competing interests of the larger society. As was common in Latin America, the upper Church hierarchy remained relatively conservative, while many parish priests, especially in urban shantytowns and in poverty-stricken rural areas, had been radicalized. The archbishop of Santo Domingo, Monseñor Nicolás de Jesús López Rodríguez, was periodically called on to promote unity among elite groups in the face of political or economic crisis, and he seemed to relish that role. Meanwhile, parish priests were organizing *comunidades de base* (grass-roots Christian communities) throughout the rural areas. Without the help of the more conservative Dominican hierarchy, but with the assistance of development organizations funded by European church groups, these priests were attempting to give their communities some basic "consciousness raising" exposure to local political and economic issues.[8]

Students

Students ordinarily have had little power, but as in other countries where political institutions are weak, they have often had high visibility. Since the death of Trujillo, students have been among the most persistent and vociferous spokesmen for the economically deprived and politically repressed. All of the major student organizations have been highly nationalistic and anti-American, and all favor far-reaching socioeconomic change, with differences of degree in their willingness to advocate violence as a means of transforming the social structure.

Of the groups that emerged in the early 1960s, Fragua (literally, "forge"), inspired by the Cuban revolution, was the most prone to employ the rhetoric of violent revolution. The Christian Revolutionary University Group (BRUC) drew its inspiration from the Social Christian movement. It was spawned by PRSC, but soon grew far more militant than the party. The Democratic Socialist University Front (FUSD), originally known as the Radical Revolutionary University Front (FURR), was affiliated with the PRD. Each university organization had an affiliate at the secondary level.

In 1965 Fragua replaced BRUC as the majority group in the nationwide Federation of Dominican Students (FED). In student elections that year at the Autonomous University of Santo Domingo, Fragua candidates led, followed closely by BRUC, while FURR candidates trailed as a weak third. By 1970 the FUSD had swept university elections and was by far the strongest organization.

Students from all of these groups participated enthusiastically in the Constitutionalist struggle against the Loyalist military faction and the U.S. forces. Many of them assumed leadership roles, and students as a whole suffered more than most groups from the repression of former rebels after the rebellion was subdued. Nevertheless, throughout the late 1960s and into the early 1970s student strikes and demonstrations continued to occur frequently. Under the Balaguer government, the Autonomous University of Santo Domingo, the nation's largest uni-

---

8. Teofílio Díaz, director of projects, Centro de Planificación y Acción Ecuménica (CEPAE), interview with the author, Santo Domingo, January 9, 1985.

versity, with more than 60,000 students, was considered enemy territory. Military and police forces entered the grounds, on occasion, firing indiscriminately. Balaguer himself dared not enter the university at all. University funds were cut, and at times the university was sealed off and classes were suspended. Not surprisingly, many students were alienated from the existing political and social systems and pessimistic with regard to prospects for their own careers or for improvement in living standards for the majority.

Peace returned to the campuses with the inauguration of the PRD government in 1978, but by the mid 1980s university–government relations were once again strained. The most active and politically successful student groups continue to be those of the more radical left, affiliated with the PLD and the FID. In 1984, FID supporters gained control of the Federation of Dominican Students (FED) and elected their candidate to be rector of the university.[9]

The Armed Forces

The Dominican armed forces have always been, above all, a political force. Before the U.S. occupation (1916–1924), the military consisted of hastily armed and mobilized bands who fought on behalf of competing regional caudillos. Since that occupation, the military has served more consistently as an instrument of U.S. policy than as the instrument of any class or regional interest in the Dominican Republic. First and foremost, however, among the interests served by military power have been those of the institution itself and of its highest-ranking officers. The same might be said of the National Police, which was united with other armed bodies in the Dominican constabulary, established during the U.S. occupation. The National Police has since become a separate body in form, but in the political context it operates as a branch of the armed forces, and its senior officers are drawn from and circulated back to the other services.

The reconstituted gendarmerie that the U.S. occupation forces left behind became Trujillo's vehicle for attaining control of the government. Once in power, Trujillo used the military to crush opposition and maintain himself in power, but he stripped it of independent political influence. After the assassination of Trujillo, the military

---

9. Yvette Sabbagh, interview with the author, Santo Domingo, January 7, 1985.

6. SOCIAL SECTORS AND INTEREST GROUPS

emerged as the strongest institution in the country. The confrontations that followed were not of a clear-cut military versus civilian nature; rather, they were struggles among changing alliances of civilian and military cliques. Nevertheless, civilian leaders remained less than comfortable in dealing with military men whose acclimation to their roles had taken place under the brutalizing leadership of Trujillo. As head of government under the Triumvirate, Donald Reid Cabral once confided to a friend that he was very careful about what he said around military men. They were accustomed to taking drastic action on very subtle commands or even comments from Trujillo.[10]

During the civil war of 1965 the armed forces nearly disintegrated as an institution. Colonel Caamaño led many younger officers and several whole contingents in support of the Constitutionalist movement. After order was restored, the Loyalist leader, Wessín, having been promoted to general, and the Constitutionalist leader, Colonel Caamaño, along with several officers who fought with them, were sent abroad (exiled) to diplomatic posts. Nevertheless, the move nearly toppled the provisional government, and rumors of impending military intervention were heard throughout the 1966 election campaign.

One of the provisions of the Institutional Act, imposed after order was restored, was that the Constitutionalist forces should be reincorporated into the regular army, but that did not take place. Those of the rebels who were not imprisoned or exiled were isolated in a single base, where they remained well into the 1970s. Some Constitutionalist officers have been reintegrated, however, since the PRD returned to power.[11]

In the 1970s, the highest-ranking officers were generally engaged in power struggles among themselves, and a semblance of civilian control was maintained through the adroitness of President Balaguer in playing off one faction against another. He frequently reshuffled the top military positions. This was done to ensure that no officer gained clear ascendancy over the others or retained his command long enough to establish a personal following among his subordinates.

10. "I'm tired of so-and-so's complaints," for example, might have been taken as an order for execution (Alfonso Moreno Martínez, interview with the author, Santo Domingo, January 2, 1985).
11. In 1985, there were at least seven former Constitutionalists in responsible positions in the armed forces, including the under-secretary for the Navy, Admiral Manuel Móntes Arache.

At the same time, Balaguer was exceedingly generous with his supporters in uniform. Whereas during his first term the armed forces held one cabinet seat, they held two seats in his second term and three in his third. Promotions were accelerated, resulting in a top-heavy command structure. Whereas there had been only 6 general-rank officers on active duty when Balaguer assumed the presidency in 1966, there were 48 by the time he reluctantly stepped down in 1978.[12]

The military share of the budget also rose steadily under Balaguer, amounting, in fact, in his final years, to almost twice the appropriated figures, as funds were transferred, without legislative approval, from education and health and welfare programs into military coffers. It was estimated that actual military spending in 1977 was about $75 million, although only $42.7 million was appropriated for that purpose. Furthermore, military officers were assigned to administer state lands and industries and even welfare programs, and their use of such sinecures for personal enrichment was carefully overlooked.[13]

Little wonder that as the 1978 elections approached, the armed forces and the National Police were unhappy at the prospect of the replacement of Balaguer and the PR. They were especially unhappy at the prospect of the return to power of the PRD, which they considered a socially disruptive, if not communistic, element. Nevertheless, facing that outcome, the uniformed services were unable to present a united front. One reason was that there was intense rivalry among the officers most loyal to Balaguer, especially between General Nivar Seijas, chief of the National Police, and General Enrique Pérez y Pérez, commander of the army's First Brigade. Balaguer himself had cultivated such rivalry as a means of preventing successful conspiracy against him, but in 1978 it worked against his interest, as Pérez and others refused to follow the lead of General Nivar Seijas.

Another obstacle to military unity was widespread resentment among colonels and other field-grade officers of the corruption (or monopolization of corruption) in the upper ranks and what they saw as the stagnated promotion system. They saw little reason to put themselves at risk only to ensure the sinecures of their superiors. Officers of this persuasion, who came to be known as the Nineteenth of May Group, had begun meeting about a year before the election,

---

12. G. Pope Atkins, *Arms and Politics in the Dominican Republic* (Boulder, CO: Westview Press, 1981), p. 46.
13. *Ibid.*, pp. 107–122.

and by the time of Guzmán's inauguration counted a majority of the younger colonels and lieutenant colonels in their ranks.

Finally, the politicians in uniform were stunned by the levels of domestic and external opposition to the interruption of the vote count. They had always assumed, in particular, that they could count on the backing of the U.S. military; finding, in this instance, that their ultimate base of support was not supportive was a frustrating and sobering experience. In the end, the conspirators remained a minority faction, and as pressure mounted and Balaguer vacillated they withdrew, claiming that there had never been a coup plot and that nothing out of the ordinary had happened.

As a fallback position, with the obliging assistance of the PR-dominated Congress, the armed forces sought to insulate themselves from civilian control through legislation before the PRD government assumed power. Legislation passed in the lame-duck session raised military pay; directed the Department of National Investigation (DNI) (a secret police and intelligence unit often used by Balaguer to repress the PRD) to report to the secretary of the armed forces rather than to the president; stipulated that the armed forces secretary must have been a major general for at least 5 years; and provided that officers could not be transferred by civilian authorities before they had served 2 years in a given post. Balaguer then reshuffled and further promoted his loyalists so that each of them would have a full 2 years to serve before Guzmán could move them.

As the ultimate insult to the incoming civilian government, the *comedores económicos*, or "soup kitchens," for the urban poor were transferred to the jurisdiction of the armed forces. This was done so that Major General Melido Marte Pichardo, Balaguer's presidential security chief, who had been administering the program, could continue to use it for his personal enrichment.

Even those senior officers who had been hesitant to participate in the abortive election-day coup were prepared to give Guzmán no more than a 6-month probationary period, and it appeared that the PR's eleventh-hour legislation had indeed placed Guzmán on a short leash. But Guzmán managed to turn the tables. Strengthened by an intensely antimilitary popular mood at home and by continued support from Washington, Guzmán disregarded the tainted legislation and moved quickly to rid his government of those officers who most clearly threatened it. Nivar Seijas and Pérez y Pérez, who had been linked, in the early 1970s, to death-squad activities, were among the 23 senior officers retired in short order. More than 240 potentially disloyal commissioned and noncommissioned officers were also replaced by more reliable ones.

The armed forces did not necessarily accept Guzmán's initiatives with good grace. In fact, a coup was plotted in 1979, but Guzmán was able to crush it before it unfolded. In the meantime, his promotions of junior and middle-ranking officers who had been dead-ended or derailed by Balaguer boosted morale among that long-disgruntled set and attenuated their hostility to the PRD.

Jorge Blanco, portrayed by Guzmán himself as a leftist, was even less acceptable to politically oriented officers than Guzmán had been. Having so much to overcome, Jorge Blanco has been exceptionally generous with the military. Salaries have been raised, and housing facilities and commissary offerings expanded. A new Social Security Institute, including a hospital, has been established exclusively for the armed forces and the police. Jet planes and modern patrol boats have been purchased, and extralegal enterprises have been overlooked.

Nevertheless, Jorge Blanco has never achieved the levels of control over, and respect from, the officer corps that Guzmán enjoyed. In fact, they simply refused to accept his first choice for commander of the army; he was forced to back down and withdraw his nominee and to accept General José Ernesto Cruz Brea, reputedly a right-wing hardliner, in that position.[14]

The PRD governments have attempted to depoliticize the armed forces. Officers charged with attempting to influence votes during the last election were reprimanded. Nevertheless, the secretary of state for the armed forces, General Manuel Antonio Cuervo Gómez, reputed to be highly professional, issued a strong warning to the left in an interview published in November 1984.[15]

The fierce factionalism of the 1970s has not reappeared. Nor has there appeared a new center for political intrigue comparable to the CEFA of the 1960s. Some critics contend that military officers are too busy getting rich to want to bother with politics. Even in the 1980s

---

14. Cruz Brea studied law in Paris and is said to have developed a fascination with Napoleon. He was a close associate of General Pérez y Pérez at the time when the latter was directing La Banda. Even political moderates describe Cruz Brea as "Nazi-like" or "fascist."
15. Colonel Wayne Wheeler, U.S. military attaché, and Lieutenant Bob Brown, staff member, attaché office, U.S. Embassy, interview with author, Santo Domingo, January 9, 1985.

there were unsolved murders that many attributed to the armed forces and the police, but such murders were not necessarily political; some appeared to be related to drug trafficking and illegal currency-exchange operations. Following the kidnap−murder of a prominent banker, Héctor Mendes, in January 1985, General Ramiro Matos González, minister of interior and police, dismissed the National Police chief and assumed that position himself. Witnesses had alleged that Mendes was kidnapped by the police.

Leaders of the PRD maintain that civilian control over the armed forces has been institutionalized, but they clearly prefer not to test that hypothesis. They remain particularly concerned about the extent of U.S. training of Dominican officers.[16] All of the country's military cadets train at U.S. schools in Panama, and some two dozen high-ranking Dominican officers are graduates of the U.S. Army Command and General Staff School. The Dominican armed forces opened their own command and general staff school in 1984, modeled on its U.S. counterpart. The republic also has an elite unit known as the *Cazadores de la Montaña* (Highland Rangers), trained by U.S. specialists in counterinsurgency, which trains other services.

Colonel Wayne Wheeler, U.S. miliary attaché in Santo Domingo, told me that the relationship between the Dominican armed forces and their U.S. counterparts is closer than that of any other Latin American military establishment. "Even their uniforms," he says, "are copies of ours."[17]

---

16. Winston Arnaud, interview with the author, January 10, 1985.
17. Wheeler, interview.

7
THE DOMINICAN REPUBLIC IN INTERNATIONAL POLITICS

The republic's foreign policies and external relationships have always been inextricably intertwined with domestic political competition. Nationalism has been undermined by the perceived requirements of national or factional self-preservation. Attempts have been made on various occasions throughout Dominican history to exchange national sovereignty for security under the flag of Colombia, France, Spain, England, or the United States. But, like "democracy," national independence has become a highly valued ideal, to such an extent that even those who profited from the U.S. intervention in 1965 felt compelled to criticize it, and foreign companies with large-scale investments attempt to maintain a low profile.

Aside from the intermittent friction in the country's relations with Haiti, which date back to the early nineteenth century, the Dominican role in international affairs in the twentieth century has been a function of the nature of its government and of ties with the United States. The interests of the United States, as perceived by Dominican leaders, have determined the latitude within which Dominican policies might fluctuate. Within that latitude, however, there has been room for considerable variation. The authoritarian government of Trujillo maintained close ties with other authoritarian governments. The Bosch government cultivated ties with governments whose leaders had been chosen in free elections. While eschewing diplomatic ties with socialist countries, the Balaguer government tended not to differentiate in its relations between authoritarian and democratic governments under capitalist systems. The return to power of the PRD has meant a renewed emphasis on ties with democratic governments.

Domestic Correlates of Foreign Policy

Opting for Protection over Sovereignty

The experience of incursions from Haiti, beginning at the turn of the nineteenth century, and of occupation by Haitian forces from 1822 to 1844 left the republic's economic and political elites with an irrepressible sense of insecurity. That generalized insecurity had much to do with the willingness of nineteenth-century leaders to exchange the trappings of sovereignty for protection by some stronger state.

It was not merely consideration of the security interests of Dominicans as a whole, however, or even of Dominican elites, that prompted leaders to forfeit, or seek to forfeit, national independence; it was also the "security" interests and ambitions of individuals and factions. No actual or aspiring leaders had a genuinely national base of support, but it was generally those factions and leaders having less popular support than their rivals who sought foreign support for their own claims to leadership. Thus, for more than four decades after liberation from Haitian control, Generals Santana and Báez, competing militarily between themselves and against other, more nationalistic, factions, treated the national territory like so much real estate to be awarded to the highest bidder.

Santana, in enticing the Spanish to return in 1861, secured for himself the position of Captain General of the colony. In 1870, after Santana's death and the defeat and departure of the Spanish, Báez, competing with the "Blues," who had led the struggle for liberation from Spain, negotiated a treaty of annexation with the United States. The treaty was rejected by the U.S. Senate, but Báez proceeded in 1872 to lease the Samaná peninsula to a New York corporation.

The lease was canceled by Báez's successor. Ulises Heureaux, who ruled autocratically from 1882 until his assassination in 1899, also negotiated for the lease of Samaná to the United States, but a storm of protest when the agreement became known obliged him to rescind it. Having sunk the country deeply into debt, Heureaux even made a secret treaty with Haiti to sell off a slice of Dominican territory along the border.[1]

The Dominican Republic's mounting debts to European powers as well as to the United States, together with the increasingly expansion-

---

1. Bell, *The Dominican Republic* (Boulder, CO: Westview Press, 1981).

ist mood of the United States, led to the establishment in the Dominican Republic of the U.S. customs receivership in 1905. Though the establishment of the receivership prompted no general insurrection, the move was so unpopular in the Dominican Republic that it was accompanied by chronic political chaos. The republic suffered at least 10 presidents and innumerable conspiracies and abortive coups between 1900, when the first steps were taken toward the establishment of the receivership, and 1916, when the direct U.S. occupation began.

The Frustration of Nascent Nationalism

Intervention by the United States had in part generated the chaos that in turn became the rationale and justification for more direct intervention. But Dominicans, having repeatedly fought for liberation from some foreign occupier only to see their own leaders bring the foreigners back, had developed intensely nationalistic sentiments. No Dominican leader was willing, in this case, to serve as a puppet president, and the United States was forced to rule directly by martial law.

Those Dominicans who believed that they had rid themselves of U.S. domination in 1924 were soon to be disappointed. The constabulary-cum-Dominican-Army, created by the U.S. occupation forces, remained the decisive force in Dominican politics, and its commander, Rafael Trujillo, soon established a dictatorship as enduring and brutal as any the hemisphere had seen. If the Trujillo regime was a vehicle for the maintenance of U.S. control over the republic, Trujillo was nevertheless no mere puppet. He was a manipulator of the first order, who used his links with the hegemonic power to great personal advantage. The United States, in some ways, became a hostage to the Frankenstein it had created.

Trujillo's foremost concern in foreign affairs, as in domestic affairs, was retaining his grip on power. The first requirement for retaining power was to stay in the good graces of the United States. At the same time he sought to increase his own room for maneuver by loosening the grip of the United States on Dominican state revenues. In 1940 he secured an end to the customs convention, and in the mid 1940s he retired the public debt owed to the United States. Until the mid 1950s, when he began in earnest to build his own sugar empire, he was solicitous of U.S. foreign investment.

During World War II, Trujillo declared war on the Axis powers and granted the United States naval bases. When the cold war developed, he severed relations with the Soviet Union and proclaimed himself the world's "Number One Anticommunist." He signed a Point Four Agreement for technical assistance with the United States and granted the United States missile-tracking sites. In 1953, the Dominican Republic became the first Latin American state to sign a bilateral Mutual Defense Assistance Agreement with the United States. Under its terms, Trujillo's armed forces received both weapons and training. Having learned early on, however, how the United States was able to use the armed forces to its own purposes, Trujillo never allowed any U.S. officer to visit a barracks without his permission.[2]

Trujillo tried to subvert Premier Fidel Castro's Cuban government until 1960, when United States and OAS hostility toward both the Cuban and Dominican regimes induced a tacit truce. The Dominican voting record in the United Nations paralleled that of the United States more closely than did the record of any other Latin American government. For further insurance of continuing U.S. backing, Trujillo employed prominent U.S. citizens to lobby the U.S. government in his behalf.

Despite such precautions, Trujillo, by the late 1950s, was losing U.S. favor. The viciousness with which he repressed dissent had become an embarrassment to U.S. officials. Furthermore, he was constantly embroiled in political disputes and paramilitary skirmishes elsewhere in the Caribbean and in Central America. His regime was a party to 12 of the 24 disputes calling for mediation by the Organization of American States between 1958 and 1960. His attempt on the life of Rómulo Bétancourt, president of Venezuela, was the last straw for the OAS members, who in 1960 voted to sever diplomatic relations with the republic and impose an economic embargo. In fact, the outrage against Trujillo in the hemisphere was such that U.S. officials concluded it would be difficult to persuade OAS members to move against Castro as long as Trujillo remained in power.

For those and other reasons, the United States decided that Trujillo had outlived his usefulness. When it became clear that the United States had turned against him, Trujillo, always the pragmatist, sought protection from the Soviet Union, but his efforts were in vain.

2. Winston Arnaud, interview with the author, Santo Domingo, January 10, 1985. It might be for that reason, in part, that the United States was left with no alternative to assassination for getting rid of Trujillo.

7. THE DOMINICAN REPUBLIC IN INTERNATIONAL POLITICS

Relations with the United States

While Dominican independence in the nineteenth century was twice suppressed and always vulnerable, no single pretender to hegemony over the new republic remained long unchallenged. Spain, France, Haiti, Great Britain, and the United States each sought, over extended periods, to influence or control events in the republic and to frustrate the advances of other pretenders, if not to occupy and colonize. But since the turn of the twentieth century, U.S. suzerainty over the republic has been unchallenged in the international arena. The only serious challenge to U.S. pretensions has come from the Dominican people themselves.

Variation in U.S. policy over the long term has had more to do with style and capability than with basic orientation. The pretensions of the United States with regard to the whole of Latin America were expressed as early as 1823 in the Monroe Doctrine. The doctrine declared that any attempt on the part of the European countries to extend their power systems to any portion of the Western Hemisphere would be considered dangerous to the peace and safety of the United States. At that time the United States had neither the willingness to make binding commitments nor the wherewithal to protect or control its southern neighbors. But the doctrine was important as the germ of what was to become a more ambitious policy when the United States became a regional and, later, a global power.

By the turn of the twentieth century, the United States, emboldened by its victory over Spain in what John Hay had dubbed the "splendid little war," had become infected with an urge for empire. The Monroe Doctrine was dusted off and embellished with the Roosevelt Corollary, which assumed the right and duty of the United States to exercise an international police power over its unruly neighbors in Central America and the Caribbean.

Unlike its original version, this new expanded doctrine was no idle threat. The customs receivership established in the Dominican Republic in 1905 and the 1916–1924 marine occupation were part of a larger pattern, which included the liberation of Panama from Colombia and the consolidation of control, through treaties, customs receiverships, and/or military occupation over Panama, Cuba, Haiti, and Nicaragua. These measures, along with occasional military interventions elsewhere and gunboat and dollar diplomacy, served to keep the Caribbean Basin states submissive in the short term, but also, in some cases, to sow the seeds of revolution.

In the Dominican Republic, as elsewhere, nationalism began to take the form of resentment against this new hegemonic power. And there, as elsewhere, U.S. decision makers have been inclined to view such nationalism as a manifestation of foreign influence. The threat from Germany had been among the rationales for the marine occupation; and marine officers, especially those in intelligence, tried ceaselessly to prove that the Germans had instigated the peasant uprising in the east. They claimed that the "bandits" were funded and armed by Germany and even that their attacks were coordinated with German offensives in Europe.[3]

Some two decades later, U.S. support for the villainous Trujillo was justified by the threat from Germany, and, once Germany was defeated, it was justified by the threat from the Soviet Union. The Soviet Union and its offshoot "communist menace" have continued to be the focal points of U.S. strategic concerns, dramatized by the list of 58 communists President Johnson used to justify the marine occupation of 1965–1966.

As nationalism in the Dominican Republic has grown, nurtured by education, urbanization, and the development of a modern political party (the PRD), so, too, has the perception on the part of U.S. officials of a security threat and of the need to maintain a veto over policy and the selection of policymakers in the republic. Thus Dominican nationalism and the U.S. compulsion to maintain control are mutually reinforcing, generating increasing volatility.

The Dominican Role in U.S. History

While the United States looms large in Dominican history, the Dominican Republic has also acquired a special place—albeit a place unappreciated by most Dominicans—in U.S. history. The republic's small size and population, its proximity to the United States, its poverty, and the insecurity of its elites have made it more readily manipulable than most countries and thus a choice testing or proving ground for new initiatives in U.S. policy.

From Teddy Roosevelt with his "big stick" and Woodrow Wilson

---

3. Bruce J. Calder, *The Impact of Intervention: The Dominican Republic during the U.S. Occupation of 1916–1924* (Austin: University of Texas Press, 1984), p. 131.

7. THE DOMINICAN REPUBLIC IN INTERNATIONAL POLITICS

with his misguided missionary zeal to Jimmy Carter with his human rights policy, U.S. presidents have found it easier to demonstrate their individuality and their departures from the policies of their predecessors through foreign policy rather than domestic policy and in small, weak, and nearby states rather than in large, strong, and distant ones. Largely frustrated in their efforts to leave their marks on the unwieldy United States, U.S. presidents have nevertheless readily left their marks on the Dominican Republic.

Whether or not the United States should continue to exercise the control implicit in a hegemonic relationship is a question that has not been openly raised by any U.S. administration since the country's Western Hemisphere sphere of influence began to be demarcated. The only remaining question has been whether or not the United States would assume the responsibilities implicit in a colonial relationship. In that sense, liberal presidents have generally been more nearly colonialist than conservative ones, more likely to offer carrots along with sticks. Whereas conservative presidents have generally limited their concerns to the protection of U.S. investments and other economic interests and the prevention of "destabilizing" political developments, liberal presidents have sometimes promoted—at least during their first years in office—democratizing and egalitarian reforms.

Dominicans, even more than most Latin Americans, have regularly been caught in a vise as U.S. policy has shifted from one U.S. administration to the next. The PRD, encouraged in its early organizational efforts by President John F. Kennedy as a manifestation of the democratizing thrust of his Alliance for Progress, was almost crushed by President Lyndon Johnson, who chose the Dominican Republic as the arena in which to demonstrate his determination to prevent the development of "another Cuba." Balaguer and his coterie of corrupt generals, having basked in U.S. favor during the administrations of Johnson, Nixon, and Ford, were stunned to find that President Carter seriously expected them to honor the election returns of 1978. The Carter administration's timely show of force after the military and police intervened to stop the vote count proved to have been the boldest and most successful demonstration of its commitment to human rights. The PRD, in power again since that time, treads lightly now, as the human rights policy has been abandoned in favor of the Reagan administration's pursuit of cold-war confrontations.

The U.S. Role in Dominican History

It would be difficult to identify a single major development in twentieth-century Dominican history that could be explained in its entirety without reference to the policies or actions of the United States. No country in the Western Hemisphere has been more firmly locked into the U.S. sphere of influence than the Dominican Republic, and in no country of the area has the course of events been more strongly influenced by residence in that sphere.

The United States maintained direct control of Dominican customs, the primary source of government revenue, and thus of its economic relations with other countries throughout most of the first half of the twentieth century. During the years of occupation by the U.S. Marines, martial-law administration changed the laws governing land tenure so as to abolish communal holdings and facilitate land concentration in areas suited to sugar production. Legal reforms of the period also opened up land to foreign ownership and revised tariff laws so as to benefit foreign manufacturers and importers and discourage domestic enterprise.

Occupation forces also broke the power of regional bosses and centralized power in the constabulary they created. Through that constabulary, the United States gave rise to the Trujillo dictatorship, and 31 years later, when that dictatorship had become an embarrassment and an obstacle to U.S. goals, the United States ended it.

After the assassination of Trujillo, President Kennedy stationed U.S. naval units offshore near Santo Domingo until Trujillo's puppet president, Joaquín Balaguer, announced that he would liberalize the regime. By mid November, Balaguer had secured U.S. sponsorship of a resolution to lift OAS sanctions. When Trujillo's family attempted a coup d'état, the United States withdrew this resolution, again dispatched naval units, and made it clear that troops would be landed if the Trujillos did not depart. In early December, U.S. officials directly entered the stalled domestic negotiations, which eventually produced a Council of State as the executive organ of government.

The council was immediately recognized by the United States, which intervened to protect it against several attempted military coups. The United States lifted its restrictions on the importation of Dominican products, promised to increase its sugar purchases, and supplied military and technical assistance. The council entered into a bilateral agreement favorable to U.S. enterprises, and, after a strong

Dominican presentation, the United States adopted a sugar act more favorable to the country than the bills that had been proposed. Alliance for Progress funds, which had been extended previously on an emergency basis, were increased in an announced effort to make the republic a showcase. By the end of 1962, three times the Latin American per capita average in foreign aid funds had been allocated by the United States to the Dominican Republic.

The more complex system of parties, unions, and other social, economic, and political organizations that arose from the debris of the Trujillo dictatorship was also heavily influenced by U.S. government and private interests. Acting on behalf of the White House, with CIA funds, Sacha Volman led efforts to organize a rural base for the PRD and became a major Bosch confident, while the AIFLD, also funded in part by the CIA, was organizing a major urban union, CONATRAL, to parallel and weaken the PRD's urban union base. Meanwhile, U.S. military and police programs were training and funding counterinsurgency and internal security forces who saw all reformists as communists and who would soon conspire to crush the showcase democracy President Kennedy had greeted with much fanfare.

Like other liberal governments, the Kennedy administration often seemed to be pulling in opposite directions at the same time. This was in part because the liberals felt constrained to cater to the fears of more conservative elements both in the government itself and in the private sector and in part because the White House was not in full control of the bureaucracy. Kennedy administration liberals even felt obliged to explain basically humanitarian policies in traditional strategic terms. Democracy and economic reform were being promoted, they said, as a more effective shield than dictatorship against communism.

The Johnson administration, more conservative in foreign policy, did just the opposite. The Dominican intervention of 1965, motivated by traditional economic and strategic concerns, was first justified, for public consumption, as a humanitarian gesture: to rescue Americans whose lives were threatened by the civil strife. But Johnson was hard put to find an American who could claim to have felt threatened *before* the marines landed and full-scale hostilities broke out.

Once that rationale had lost its usefulness, Johnson claimed that the country was threatened with a communist takeover. To prove his point, he produced his flawed list of 58 communists in the Constitutionalist movement.

The "invitation" to intervene in the Dominican Republic came from so-called government forces, even though the de facto government had already fallen and the Constitutionalists were in control of most of the capital. In fact, those "government forces" were a motley crew of military officers assembled largely by the U.S. Embassy for the purpose of appearing to have a "government" to defend.

The intervention resulted in several thousand deaths, in a reinforcement of anti-Americanism among Dominicans, and in the reinstatement of much of the political infrastructure of the Trujillo era. In the aftermath of intervention, the Johnson administration, seeking to prop up the new government of Balaguer, to demonstrate that the intervention had been beneficial to the republic, and to smooth the way for U.S. investors, raised U.S. assistance to unprecedented levels.

The ill will engendered by the intervention of the Johnson administration, and by Nixon administration support for the Balaguer regime through its most repressive years, was assuaged to some extent by the initiatives of the Carter administration on behalf of respect for democracy and human rights. Nevertheless, U.S. insistence on the isolation of Cuba and on security and benefits for U.S. investors, along with U.S. policies on trade, aid, and credit, continued to frustrate Dominican governments and Dominican nationalists.

In the mid 1980s, in conjunction with routine matters of trade and aid, the U.S. government remained heavily involved in efforts to influence policy and policymaking processes. A loan, for example, of $41 million, extended by USAID in 1982 to cover the balance of payments on Dominican imports of U.S. goods and services, required matching funds in Dominican pesos to finance programs jointly monitored by the U.S. and Dominican governments. USAID's balance-of-payments support agreement for 1983 specified that aid mission members would meet regularly with Dominican government officials to discuss national economic issues and would have access to government financial data. The agreement also noted that U.S. loans were to be conditional on Dominican acceptance of the IMF's austerity program.

The United States and the IMF have pressured the Dominican government to abandon the vestiges of import substitution industry; to concentrate on export production; and to increase credit and infrastructural support for agro-industry, mining, tourism, and industrial free zones. USAID has strongly urged the government to cut back on social service programs and to abandon protective tariffs.[4]

The U.S. Embassy has also sponsored efforts to advise or train Dominican political leaders in campaign and electoral procedures and in the functions of political parties and congressional representatives. In particular, U.S. advisers discouraged party discipline and advocated an individualistic approach to representation. In this, U.S. advisers sometimes found themselves at cross-purposes with European—particularly West German—advisers.[5]

Finally, to the distress of some PRD leaders, the United States maintained its monopoly on the training of Dominican military officers. U.S. military personnel on full-time duty in the republic in 1985 were limited to three in the attaché's office and six in the Military Assistance Advisory Group. But all of the republic's military cadets train at U.S. facilities in Panama, and high-ranking Dominican officers are routinely accommodated at the U.S. Command and General Staff School.[6]

Relations with Haiti

Tension has generally run high between Haiti and the Dominican Republic since the Dominicans gained their independence in 1844, after 22 years of Haitian occupation. Legends growing out of the occupation have kept fears and racial animosity alive in the Dominican Republic. The most serious incident between the two countries in the twentieth century was the massacre in 1937 by the Dominican Army, under the Trujillo government, of an unknown number (Haiti claimed 12,000; the Dominican Republic claimed 18,000; other estimates run as high as 25,000 to 30,000) of Haitians, mostly seasonal agricultural workers, in the Dominican Republic.[7]

Leaders in each country have habitually attempted to influence

---

4. Tom Barry, Beth Wood, and Deb Preusch; *The Other Side of Paradise: Foreign Control in the Caribbean* (New York: Grove Press, 1984), pp. 292–301; Marion Ford, AID, confirmed that he placed high priority on discouraging government "giveaway" programs and on promoting agro-export industries.
5. Julio Brea Franco, dean of the College of Social Sciences, Technological Institute of Santo Domingo, interview with the author, Santo Domingo, January 7, 1985.
6. Wayne Wheeler, interview with the author, Santo Domingo, January 9, 1985.
7. Haiti's president was paid off by Trujillo to downplay the incident.

internal political struggles in the other; and political exiles and refugees, with or without the complicity of sympathetic governments, have kept the island seething with plots and rumors of plots. Since World War II, however, disputes between the two countries have been mitigated by the intercession of the OAS. The second application of the Inter-American Treaty of Reciprocal Assistance (commonly known as the Rio Treaty, 1947) took place in response to charges of aggression brought by Haiti against the Dominican Republic, together with countercharges by the latter against Haiti, Cuba, and Guatemala. Haiti first appealed to the OAS in 1949, claiming that the activities of a former Haitian army officer, who had taken asylum in the Dominican Republic, endangered the peace, but the OAS council determined that the circumstances did not warrant recourse to the collective-security treaty. Haiti then turned to the Inter-American Peace Committee, which was able to smooth over the immediate crisis.

Within a year, the situation had deteriorated again, and the charges and countercharges indicated to the OAS council a clear threat to the peace. An investigating committee, dispatched by the council, discovered the complicity of the Dominican government in a plot against Haiti, as well as of the governments of Cuba and Guatemala in plots against the Dominican Republic. Owing to the complexity of the situation, a continuing special committee was appointed to try to defuse crises as they arose. It was assumed that the exposure of extralegal activities on the part of several governments had the effect of deflating the whole movement of political subversion.

Trujillo, since assuming power in 1930, had habitually attempted to eliminate Haitian presidents who were neither fearful of him nor dependent on him, and during Francois Duvalier's first year as Haitian president, the two men were bitter rivals. They soon realized, however, that antiauthoritarian forces throughout the Caribbean were seeking to overthrow both of them, so in 1958 they signed a mutual-assistance pact, the Agreement of Malpasse.

Relations became tense again after the assassination of Trujillo in 1961, and especially after the election of Juan Bosch to the presidency of the Dominican Republic in 1962. In 1963 Bosch's government appealed to the OAS alleging the forcible entrance of the Dominican Embassy in Port-au-Prince—in pursuit of Haitian dissidents who had taken asylum there—as one of many acts by the Haitian government that endangered the peace. The machinery of the Rio Treaty was set in motion, and a committee authorized to carry out conciliatory, as well as investigative, functions was sent to the island. Charges and countercharges mounted, and the Haitian government rejected the recommendations of the committee. Meanwhile, Bosch moved Dominican troops to the border. Although no clashes took place between the armed forces of the two countries, disturbing incidents continued, and the OAS council left the case on the books until August 1966.[8]

After Bosch was deposed, the Triumvirate's efforts to resume relations with Haiti failed, and border incidents, which resulted in Dominican mobilization and Haitian charges before the United Nations, occurred in 1964. A year later, Haiti alleged that the Constitutionalists were preparing an invasion. Haiti resumed diplomatic relations with the Dominican Republic after the election of Balaguer to the Dominican presidency in 1966. Since that time, relations between the two countries have generally been correct, although disparaging or threatening remarks have occasionally been exchanged, and the border between the two countries has been closed part of the time.

Since the death in 1971 of Francois ("Papa Doc") Duvalier, Haiti's ruler for the previous 13½ years, the Haitian and Dominican governments have entered into agreements to facilitate and expand trade between their countries. Agreements signed in 1972 provided for the establishment of a joint free zone; reduced tariffs and simplified trade transactions; and called for improvements in transportation.

More recently, tensions between the two countries have been exacerbated by the widening gap in development—stagnation in Haiti while the Dominican economy has experienced spurts of growth. This has increased the incentive for Haitians to cross the border, legally or otherwise, in search of work. Dominicans are resentful and fearful of the Haitian migration, while Haitians resent the discrimination and conditions of near servitude to which their countrymen are subjected on the other side.

A UN study, citing an agreement between the two governments on fees paid for each Haitian worker sent to the Dominican Republic, was condemnatory of both governments. It alleged that some 12,000 Haitian cane cutters were leased annually to Dominicans for $11 a head

---

8. Although Bosch has disavowed it, some Dominican leaders believe that the dispute with Haiti was the surface manifestation of a plan spawned by Bosch and the Kennedy White House to support an invasion of Haiti by exiles seeking to topple Papa Doc. Vincho Castillo says that a boat used during that crisis by Haitian exiles had been purchased from a friend of his by a member of Bosch's cabinet.

and that in Dominican labor camps those workers lived in conditions of extreme squalor and depravity.[9]

The Guzmán government made a concerted effort to expand commerce with Haiti and to mitigate racial and cultural antagonisms. Guzmán and Haitian president Jean Claude ("Baby Doc") Duvalier met in 1979 and signed an agreement of cooperation. They met again later to open a new irrigation project benefiting both countries. More recently, the two governments created a fund of $1 million to be used for trade promotion. In the early 1980s it was apparent that trade between the two countries was increasing somewhat, but it remained very low as a percentage of total Dominican exports and imports. Border crossing points between the two countries generally remained closed.

Cautiously Expanding Horizons

The Dominican Republic has traditionally maintained a low profile in world affairs, except when the villainy of Trujillo or the interventions of the United States have dragged it unwillingly into the spotlight. Its international contacts have been limited in part by the country's small size and limited resources. The maintenance of embassies and the promotion of regional or global schemes are, after all, expensive endeavors.

The republic's contacts have been limited also by domestic tyranny and turmoil. Trujillo and, to a lesser degree, Balaguer saw international travel and the maintenance of foreign contacts by private Dominican citizens as potentially threatening to their versions of political stability. Nor was the tumult of the period between those regimes conducive to external initiatives.

Finally, the republic's international contacts have been limited as a consequence of the nature of its relationship with the United States and of U.S. fears and predilections. The United States has been a jealous patron. It has insisted that the Dominican Republic remain isolated from the so-called communist sphere, particularly from its neighbor, Cuba. It has even opposed Dominican efforts to expand economic ties with Western Europe.

9. Howard J. Wiarda and Michael J. Kryzanek, *The Dominican Republic: A Caribbean Crucible* (Boulder, CO: Westview Press, 1982), p. 130.

7. THE DOMINICAN REPUBLIC IN INTERNATIONAL POLITICS

Nevertheless, in marked contrast to the relative insularity of its governments and the limited nature of formal, state-to-state relations, the republic's political elite is very well traveled and well connected in the international community. Because of the long periods of tyranny, interspersed with anarchy, most Dominican political leaders have lived in exile on several occasions—most often in Venezuela and Puerto Rico, but also in Costa Rica, Mexico, Cuba, and other Latin American states, on the U.S. mainland, and in Spain, France, Great Britain, and other European countries. Dominican politicians, especially those on the left, have also sought to counterbalance the influence of their domestic opponents and of the United States by building support networks among European and Latin American socialists and social democrats. PRD leader Peña Gómez, for example, who has always had good reason for concern about opposition to his political aspirations on the part of U.S. and Dominican conservatives, has cultivated close ties with European leaders. He serves as president of the Latin American affiliate of the Socialist International, whose world president is West Germany's Willy Brandt.

Dominican relations with the outside world have, at any rate, expanded greatly since the 1960s. The republic now maintains diplomatic relations with most Latin American and Western European countries and with a few capitalist states in other parts of the world. The PRD governments have gradually expanded trade with Latin American and Caribbean states, as well as with Europe and Japan, and have even established limited commercial ties with some Soviet-bloc countries.

Relations with Latin America

In general, the republic's trade with other Latin American countries has been limited, and its most consequential interactions with other Latin American countries have taken place within the context of the OAS. Trujillo's domestic policies, restrictions on travel, and foreign intrigues tended to isolate the republic from general Latin American affairs. This isolation became more formal in 1960 when all the OAS member states that had not previously done so broke diplomatic relations. After Trujillo's assassination, many Dominicans who had developed friendships and personal interests in other Caribbean lands—particularly Puerto Rico, Venezuela, Costa Rica, and Cuba—returned from exile.

Alignment with the more authoritarian regimes of Latin America that marked the Trujillo era was reversed by President Bosch, who had been closely associated with leading Latin American liberals during his years in exile. Presidents Rómulo Bétancourt, Francisco Orlich, and Ramón Villeda Morales—of Venezuela, Costa Rica, and Honduras, respectively—attended his inauguration, as did Luis Muñoz Marín, Governor of Puerto Rico, and former Costa Rican president José Figueres. No representatives were invited from Haiti, Nicaragua, or Paraguay, and only the opposition leaders in Argentina and Peru received invitations.

In an unsuccessful attempt to avoid being deposed, Bosch appealed to the liberal leaders in 1963. Venezuela, Costa Rica, El Salvador, Honduras, and Nicaragua jointly urged nonrecognition of the Triumvirate that overthrew him. A new Honduran government, however, led in the establishment of diplomatic relations with the Triumvirate, and by October 1964 only Venezuela, Cuba, and Haiti withheld full recognition. Support for the Constitutionalist faction during the 1965 disturbances was considerable in Venezuela, Chile, Mexico, Uruguay, Peru, and Cuba, but none of these countries went so far as to extend recognition to it. The subsequent Balaguer regime maintained relations with Latin American authoritarian and democratic regimes alike, but relations with the democracies were generally less than warm.

The return to power of the PRD in 1978 was greeted enthusiastically by most Western Hemisphere states, particularly those whose governing parties, like the PRD, belonged to the Socialist International. The republic, under PRD leadership, has increased its trade with major Latin American countries, including Brazil, Mexico, and Venezuela, as well as with the larger Caribbean island states, notably Jamaica, Trinidad and Tobago, and Barbados. An agreement with Venezuela, guaranteeing uninterrupted supply and favorable loans for the purchase of oil, has been particularly helpful.

The Guzmán government became one of the first in the hemisphere to recognize Nicaragua's Sandinista government. Guzmán hailed the success of the revolution and, in a bold move, even welcomed Sandinista leaders to the Dominican Republic. The Jorge Blanco government has continued to maintain friendly relations with Nicaragua and has even expressed support for proposals—opposed by the United States—that have been set forth by the Contadora states for peaceful settlement in Central America. Neither Jorge Blanco nor Peña Gómez, however, attended the inauguration of Daniel Ortega as Nicaragua's president in January 1985.

Dominican relations with Cuba since that country's revolution have been virtually nonexistent, apart from attempts by Castro and Trujillo to undermine each other's governments. Nevertheless, the *issue* of relations with Cuba has had great symbolic importance since the 1960s, as one's stance on that issue has been seen both by U.S. officials and by Dominican nationalists as a measure of one's loyalty (or subservience) to the United States.

The Council of State that governed briefly in 1962–1963 accused Castro of attempted subversion, called for OAS sanctions, and threatened to recognize a Cuban government in exile. Bosch, after receiving complaints from U.S. officials that he had failed to mention Castro in his inaugural address, denounced communism and denied any intention to open diplomatic relations with Cuba. He did not go out of his way thereafter to criticize the Cuban Revolution, however, and some U.S. officials, as well as Dominican conservatives, accused him of being soft on Castro.

The Triumvirate crushed guerrilla activity allegedly supported by Castro in November 1963 and supported the OAS imposition of sanctions on Cuba in 1964. Cuba, in turn, accused the Triumvirate of permitting anti-Castro exiles to use Dominican territory. From the beginning of civil strife in April 1965, Constitutionalist leaders tried to disassociate their movement from Castro's verbal support, as the charge of Cuban backing was being used against them by the "loyalist" generals and the United States.

The Balaguer regime shunned all forms of contact with Cuba and regularly charged that its critics and opponents were backed by Castro. The Guzmán government, despite strong pressures from PRD leaders and constituencies, did not open diplomatic relations with Cuba. Cuban assistance at the time of the 1979 hurricane disaster was pointedly snubbed by Guzmán, though he subsequently encouraged the development of unofficial ties through cultural and scholarly exchanges and athletic contests.

Jorge Blanco, as president of the PRD, was among those who urged Guzmán to renew diplomatic relations with Cuba. Nevertheless, as president of the republic, Jorge Blanco has reconsidered. The timing, considering the presidency of Reagan and his attitude toward Cuba, did not seem favorable for such an innovation.

In the 1980s, economic adversity and the common threat posed by debt problems and IMF solutions has drawn the republic into closer association with a number of Latin American countries. In February

1985, the republic hosted a ministerial meeting of the Cartagena group, which represents the area's most deeply indebted nations. The meeting was attended by ministers from Argentina, Bolivia, Brazil, Chile, Colombia, Ecuador, Mexico, Peru, Uruguay, and Venezuela. Jorge Blanco warned the group that the debt crisis threatens the recent trend toward democratic rule in Latin America.

Relations with Other Countries

Partly in an effort to increase his domestic political alternatives, President Bosch tried to intensify relations with Europe. After his election in 1962, he visited Europe and conferred with ranking officials in West Germany, Italy, Switzerland, France, Belgium, and Great Britain. He returned to announce that the European countries had promised three times the economic assistance offered by the United States. The U.S. Embassy reacted to Bosch's initiative with concern and resentment. After his overthrow, the Triumvirate canceled the major European arrangements.

Since 1978, PRD governments have sought to strengthen relations, in particular, with the social democratic states of Europe and with political parties around the world belonging to the Socialist International. European socialists have frequently attended conferences in Santo Domingo, and PRD members have attended conferences in Europe.

The republic's most important trading partners in the early 1980s, after the United States, were the Netherlands, West Germany, and Japan. Other countries with which the republic maintains diplomatic and commercial relations include Israel, Taiwan, and South Korea.

Participation in International Organizations

The attentions of the Organization of American States have not always been welcome in the Dominican Republic, but the organization, sometimes fronting for the United States, has had a major role in Dominican history. Likewise, the Dominican Republic has had a major role in the history of the OAS, which came into being in 1948. The peacekeeping machinery of the organization was honed on cases involving allegations of aggression by or against the Dominican Republic during the Trujillo era. The Sixth Meeting of Consultation of Foreign Ministers of the OAS, which considered Venezuela's charge against

7. THE DOMINICAN REPUBLIC IN INTERNATIONAL POLITICS

Trujillo, was the first time the OAS imposed diplomatic and economic sanctions on a member state, and the episode set the precedent that was soon followed in actions against Cuba.

After Trujillo's death, the government adopted measures designed to obtain removal of OAS sanctions. It allowed increased freedom of expression, promised to hold free elections, and warned that revolution would occur if the regime was not recognized. Leaders of the developing political opposition, however, urged the OAS to retain the sanctions. When the Trujillo family fled, the government began to erase the vestiges of Trujillismo, and early in 1962 the OAS removed its sanctions. Shortly thereafter, the secretary-general of the OAS visited the country. A technical-assistance committee from the OAS helped to rewrite Dominican electoral laws and to prepare for national elections in 1962, which brought Bosch to power.

Bosch was openly critical of the OAS, but he nevertheless called for an emergency meeting of the organization in 1963 to protest a Haitian invasion of the Dominican Embassy in Port-au-Prince. He subsequently accepted settlement of the dispute through the good offices of the OAS peace commission.

If the OAS proved its worth in the settlement of disputes involving the Dominican Republic, it also proved its vulnerability to U.S. manipulation at the expense of that country. The OAS provided a fig leaf of multilateralism to the U.S. intervention of 1965. But OAS involvement came only after the invasion and after some U.S. maneuvers, within the organization, of questionable legality. The vote required to break a tie on the adoption of the U.S.-sponsored resolution creating the Inter-American Peacekeeping Force was cast by the delegate of the Dominican junta assembled and anointed a "government" by the United States. The resolution was opposed by almost all of the democratic governments of the hemisphere. Such use of the OAS to fulfill a political purpose of the United States permanently discredited the organization in the eyes of most Latin Americans. Several subsequent attempts by the United States to resurrect an OAS peacekeeping force have met with abject failure.

Despite its having been discredited in the 1960s, OAS involvement in Dominican affairs was generally welcomed in 1978 when the organization protested military seizure of the ballot boxes. An OAS team, headed by Galo Plaza, a former OAS secretary-general and former Ecuadorean president, visited the country to pressure Balaguer and his military supporters to back off. The organization's then secretary-general, Alejandro Orfila, attended the inauguration of Guzmán a few months later.

The republic's relationship with the OAS has generally overshadowed its relationship with the United Nations, of which it is also a member. Dominican governments have invoked UN assistance principally when they have failed in an approach to the OAS. For example, after the OAS repeatedly refused to lift the sanctions it had imposed in 1960, the government protested before the United Nations that responsibility for the attempted assassination of President Bétancourt rested exclusively with Trujillo, not with the Dominican government.

Originally convened at the request of the Soviet Union, the UN Security Council discussed the civil strife and U.S. and OAS intervention in the spring of 1965. In mid-May the Constitutionalists asked the UN secretary-general to stop the advance of OAS troops beyond an international security zone it had established in the city of Santo Domingo and requested the dispatch of the UN Human Rights Commission. The Security Council, which heard delegates from the rival factions, called for a cease-fire and directed the secretary-general to send a special observer, an initiative that was promptly denounced by the faction opposing the Constitutionalists and by the OAS.

The republic also maintains membership in most of the affiliate organizations of the OAS and the United Nations, as well as in a number of international financial institutions, including the Inter-American Development Bank, the World Bank, and the International Monetary Fund. As noted, the IMF has been a major and, in general, highly unpopular actor in the domestic political arena in the 1980s.

Seeing little to be gained through participation in regional economic integration schemes, the republic opted against membership in the now defunct Latin American Free Trade Association and the Central American Common Market, as well as in the surviving Caribbean Community. It has subscribed, however, to the would-be producer cartels represented by the international bauxite and sugar agreements.

8

THE NEW ERA OF PRD RULE: POLICIES AND POLITICS

The Presidency of Guzmán

Antonio Guzmán assumed the mantle of his presidency on August 16, 1978, with high hopes and lofty ambitions and with several strikes against him. He sought to rein in runaway corruption, to promote economic growth and modernization, to provide long-neglected social services, and to accomplish all this within an environment of democracy and respect for human rights unknown since the brief tenure of the PRD in 1963.

At the same time, Guzmán was confronted with an obstructionist, PR-dominated Senate, legacy of the Balaguerist Central Election Board's brazenly creative rulings. He was dealt an economy on a sharp decline. The sugar market had gone limp, and most other exports were in low demand as well. Petroleum, all of which had to be imported, was scarce and expensive.

In the realm of partisan politics, Guzmán's position was tenuous. He lacked the charisma and personal popularity of Juan Bosch and the cunning of Balaguer. While Guzmán's reputation for moderation and pragmatism had attracted multiclass support, that reputation also generated skepticism among some leaders and constituencies of his own program-oriented party.

Finally, he took office under the shadow of a military hierarchy—locked in place by legislation passed by the lame-duck PR Congress—that was, at best, unfriendly. Even those upper-echelon officers who had been unenthusiastic about the prospects of an election-day coup were willing to give him a probationary period of no more than 6 months.

Taming the Military

Guzmán tackled his most threatening problem—the unfriendly military—with such speed and single-mindedness that it surprised even his most loyal supporters. Taking advantage of the presence of a throng of dignitaries, representing 52 states and 3 international organizations, and including, not coincidentally, the commander-in-chief of the U.S. Southern Command, he made his first moves on inauguration day. In his inaugural address, he pledged to launch a program of "depoliticization, institutionalization, and professionalization" of the armed forces and the National Police. Before the day was over, he had dismissed several senior officers who had been implicated in the abortive election-day coup. Within a few weeks of the inauguration, he had changed the entire command structure of the armed forces. Before the end of the 6 months that might have been his "probationary period," he had broken the power of the *Balaguerista* officer cliques and gained personal control over the military establishment.[1]

Guzmán's manner of dealing with his legislative straitjacket vis-à-vis the military was simple and traditional: He ignored it. Having two competing Balaguerista factions to deal with also made it possible for him to use the "divide and conquer" approach—to isolate one group at a time without great risk that they would unit against him.

The new president moved first against Major General Neit Nivar Seijas, the bête noir of the PRD. Nivar was relieved of his command of the army's First Brigade on inauguration day and was soon "exiled" to Washington, D.C. as the Dominican representative to the Inter-American Defense Board. Several months later, Nivar's brother was forcibly retired from the army and his son from the police. Nivar himself was recalled and retired in 1980.

Others relieved on inauguration day and later retired included Lieutenant General Juan René Beauchamp Javier, secretary of state of the armed forces, and Vice Admiral Francisco Rivera Caminero, navy chief of staff. Rivera was particularly reviled by PRD activists because he had ordered the naval bombardment, during the strife of 1965, of a section of Santo Domingo held by the Constitutionalist forces. The air force chief of staff, Major General Salvador Lluberes Montas, a mem-

---

1. G. Pope Atkins, *Arms and Politics in the Dominican Republic* (Boulder, CO: Westview Press, 1981), pp. 125–155.

ber of the Pérez clique, was also relieved of his post on inauguration day but was not retired until 5 months later.

While the principal *Nivarista* officers were being cashiered, Major General Enrique Pérez y Pérez and most of his followers remained in place. Pérez continued to serve as army chief of staff until the end of September, when Guzmán appointed him ambassador to Spain. The Spanish refused to receive him, and Pérez rejected a subsequent assignment to London. He was finally retired in November 1978 after a noisy showdown with Guzmán. Vice Admiral Ramón Emilio Jiménez Reyes, a Pérez loyalist, was allowed to stay on as foreign minister until January 1980, when he resigned and retired. Some Pérez allies were retained by Guzmán and appointed to high positions once the clique had been dissolved. However, most generals and many colonels who had risen to their positions under Balaguer were forced into retirement.

Only a few of the consequent vacancies at the top of the military hierarchy were filled by officers who had served the Constitutionalist cause in 1965. The military faction that was most influential for several months following Guzmán's inauguration was the Nineteenth of May Group, which had opposed the election-day intervention. Guzmán sought the group's advice in making his early appointments. Most of the group's leaders, however, were soon sidelined in unimportant posts. An exception was Brigadier General Rafael Adriano Valdez Hilario, titular head of the Nineteenth of May Group. He served as secretary of state of the armed forces until early 1980.

Meanwhile, Guzmán's transformation of the armed forces reached deeply into the ranks. In general, in the National Police as well as in the three services, he promoted a new generation of officers whom he believed to be relatively apolitical and committed to modernizing reforms. He handled promotions and transfers personally and spent a great deal of time visiting military bases and conducting military ceremonies in the presidential palace.

Guzmán established a commission, composed of high-ranking officers, which was assigned to visit military installations throughout the country, spreading the message that the military was now to shun politics altogether. He also established a policy of periodic transfers, which was to apply to officers at all levels throughout the country. Thus he sought to end the military cacique system—the control of local politics by military bosses—that had been in effect at least since the Trujillo era.

Guzmán's moves against military tradition did not go entirely unchallenged. A coup conspiracy developed by a group of discharged army officers and some civilian PR supporters was uncovered and thwarted in October 1979. His successes, however, such as they were, may be attributed in part to the fact that he was careful not to threaten the material interests of officers and enlisted men in general, and of individual officers, even as he moved to curb their power.[2]

Guzmán applauded the substantial military pay raises provided by Balaguer between the elections of 1978 and inauguration day and appeared to share in the credit for them. The new president also continued Balaguer's practice of appointing military officers to a number of high-level government positions in areas of strictly civilian concern. Guzmán did not use enticement to corruption, as Balaguer had, as a means of coopting and controlling officers and factions, but he did manage to overlook a great deal of it. Finally, Guzmán sought no departure in economic or foreign policies that might be expected to antagonize the overwhelmingly conservative armed forces. Therein, however, lay a problem that smoldered among other sectors of the population, particularly with the working-class constituency of the PRD.

Dealing with Economic Decline

During the first 6 months of his administration, while he found it necessary to give careful and constant attention to the reorganization of the military, Guzmán allowed growing social and economic problems to go largely unattended. In his state-of-the-nation address to the National Assembly 6 months into his administration, on the 135th anniversary of independence from Haiti, he concluded that the economic situation was grave, and he pledged to give it his undivided attention in the months ahead. He began on that same day to make important changes among his economic advisers.

Following on the drop in world market prices for the country's major exports, including sugar, coffee, and nickel, the construction sector went into serious decline in 1978, aggravating already high levels of unemployment. Inflation was also high, and the country was experiencing a decline in real GNP. State enterprises, confiscated from the Trujillo family, had been decapitalized during the tenure of Balaguer,

2. *Ibid.*

8. THE NEW ERA OF PRD RULE: POLICIES AND POLITICS

subjected to graft, featherbedding, and all kinds of inefficiencies. Guzmán attempted to discourage corruption and increase efficiency in these enterprises, but with little success.

Foreign aid, which had been lavish at the outset of Balaguer's reign, was now meager. The U.S. Congress was in a less than generous mood, and the Dominican Republic, appearing politically stable, was not high on its priority list. Nevertheless, to the great disappointment of many PRD leaders, Guzmán did not move decisively to restrict the advantages enjoyed by foreign—mostly U.S.—investors. Rather, he continued to see foreign investment as an indispensable source of scarce capital. Small amounts of aid were forthcoming from Great Britain, West Germany, and Venezuela, but such aid was in the form of loans or credits rather than grants.

Early in his administration, Guzmán had doubled the minimum-wage rate, which had been frozen for 12 years under Balaguer. The increase, however, failed to cover increases in the cost of living. In general, Guzmán's approach to declining exchange earnings and rising budget deficits was an austerity program that seemed to please no one. Meanwhile, the still rising price of oil threatened to strangle the economy. In July 1979 Guzmán imposed a steep increase in its price at the pump. Taxi drivers in the capital staged a protest march and were joined by many others with unmet demands. The upshot was a violent clash between protestors and police that resulted in several deaths.

In the aftermath of that clash, particularly shocking to an administration that prided itself in its respect for human rights, Guzmán nationalized the public transportation system. That measure proved to be a popular one, and by the first anniversary of Guzmán's inauguration his popularity, which had dipped sharply in previous months, appeared to be on the rise again.

Then, at the end of August 1979—as if mother nature herself wished to test the new administration—the island was swept by the most devastating hurricane the Caribbean had seen in more than a century. Hurricane David hit the south coast and moved northward, leaving a path of debris and despair across the central and western regions before plunging on toward Florida. More than 1000 people were killed, and perhaps 10,000 were injured. Property damage was estimated at more than a billion dollars. A second hurricane, Frederick, followed closely behind the first, frustrating relief efforts.

The double assault flattened dwellings, blocked roads and irrigation canals, and wiped out crops, particularly coffee and cacao. Some villages were isolated for several weeks. Even in the capital, transportation and communication were disrupted, and the water supply was contaminated. Although precautionary measures had been taken, it took about 3 weeks for authorities to restore services and a semblance of normality, and in the interim the government was the target of much grumbling.

When Guzmán first requested of the Congress special powers to deal with the disaster, PRD senators made common cause with PR ones to reject the request. No doubt Trujillo's use of "special powers" in 1931 in the aftermath of a hurricane to launch his dictatorship had crossed their minds. The Congress later granted Guzmán special powers, however, and the authorities ultimately received some credit and appreciation for their relief efforts.

In retrospect, the performance of the government in the aftermath of the hurricanes was seen to have been remarkably efficient. The economy also proved resilient. With the boost of sharp rises in late 1979 in the prices of sugar and gold on the world market, Dominican GNP growth rates began to increase. The rising price of gold, and its increasing share, by value, of Dominican exports, brought Guzmán under strong pressures to nationalize the 6-year-old mining company known as Rosario Dominicana S.A. The Central Bank already held 46 percent of the company's shares, but in October 1979 Guzmán bought the remaining shares from two U.S. companies for U.S. $70 million. The move proved popular with the general public, although some of those well informed on mineral policy charged that the government had paid far too much for the unmined assets in the worn-out old mine.[3]

Challenging the Party Regulars

When the PRD returned to power in 1978, it was not with the clear mandate it had enjoyed briefly in the early 1960s. In the Chamber of Deputies, the PRD held 48 seats to the PR's 43; the PR controlled the Senate, with 16 seats to the PRD's 11. Although the election results had been skewed by the Central Election Board to favor the PR, they were not successfully challenged, and the PRD had to live with them.

---

3. Guido D'Alessandro, who as minister of mining and commerce in 1975–1976 had tightened national controls over Rosario's operations, believes that the government paid far more than the mine was worth because Guzman's daughter, Sonia, had invested in the company.

8. THE NEW ERA OF PRD RULE: POLICIES AND POLITICS

Provincial governors, appointed by the president, were all of the PRD, but among popularly elected mayors, the PR had a majority of 52 to the PRD's 32. The PRD, however, controlled the largest cities.

The interrupted elections of 1978 were damaging to Balaguer's personal reputation. But as economic decline drained the new government's popularity, Balaguer, still at the head of his party, began to make a comeback. Nevertheless, Guzmán's most pressing political problems during his first year in office derived from a schism in his own party. Many PRD leaders and activists, particularly the party president, Senator Jorge Blanco, and its secretary-general, the mayor of Santo Domingo, Peña Gómez, were incensed by the appointment of many nonparty people to cabinet and other high-level positions.[4]

An anomaly in his own party, Guzmán was an aristocrat and a businessman. His appointments of persons with ties to the Santiago oligarchy and with foreign business interests no doubt reflected his own background as well as his concern about maintaining good relations with the United States. The appointment of Eduardo Fernández, a former vice-president of Gulf and Western, to the presidency of the Central Bank was particularly offensive to Guzmán's PRD colleagues.

Only 4 of the 11 ministries were headed by PRD regulars. Nevertheless, although most of the top-level, policymaking positions were filled by persons Guzmán claimed to have appointed for their technical abilities, middle-level positions were filled by party leaders—would-be policymakers lacking the requisite technical skills. This topsy-turvy arrangement led to predictable problems of management, in addition to intraparty friction.

PRD leaders were also embarrassed and frustrated by Guzmán's resort to nepotism. At least 37 of his relatives were appointed to important government positions. His daughter, Sonia, who became his private secretary, and his son-in-law, who served as administrative secretary, were highly influential, especially in that they controlled access to the president.

Courting the United States

A major source of friction between Guzmán and other PRD leaders was the president's stance with regard to the United States. Guzmán,

4. Adrian Rodríguez and Deborah Huntington, "Dominican Republic—The Launching of a Democracy," *NACLA Reports on the America*, Vol. 16, No. 6, November–December 1982.

highly sensitive to the historic role of the United States in Dominican politics and to the country's economic dependency, went out of his way to accommodate the Colossus of the North. Often, however, the price of accommodating the United States, and of keeping his own military establishment at bay, was policy that ran counter to the traditional social democratic programs of his party and that offended its working-class constituency.

Other party leaders, including Jorge Blanco and Peña Gómez, were disappointed that Guzmán failed to impose new restrictions on the operations of foreign companies and to nationalize certain key industries. The president's public snubbing of emergency aid from Cuba in the aftermath of the hurricane disaster was also seen as undignified cowing to the United States. Guzmán was unwilling to risk losing the more substantial U.S. disaster relief; however, the 200 U.S. servicemen sent in to assist in the relief effort caused widespread unease among PRD members old enough to remember the 1965–1966 occupation.

A more consequential move to accommodate the United States was the dismissal, in mid-1980, of Armed Forces Secretary of State Valdez Hilario and his replacement by General Mario Alfredo Imbert McGregor. The dismissal followed a visit by U.S. Army Major General Robert L. Schweitzer, who offered U.S. assistance to the Dominican military in dealing with the "communist menace." General Valdez Hilario suggested publicly that he saw no serious "menace" in the Dominican Republic and that, should one appear, Dominicans could deal with it without outside help.[5]

General Imbert McGregor is a nephew of the ambitious and ubiquitous Major General Antonio Imbert Barrera, whose close ties with U.S. military and intelligence officials date back to the assassination of Trujillo. General Imbert Barrera had become a confidant of Guzmán during the early months of Guzmán's administration. His two nephews, both in the air force, had been steadily promoted under Guzmán. Colonel Alfredo Segundo Imbert McGregor, older brother of the armed forces secretary of state, had become air force chief of staff. With those appointments, the Imberts and their allies had become the most powerful faction in the Dominican military.

---

5. Atkins, *Arms and Politics in the Dominican Republic*, pp. 145–147.

8. THE NEW ERA OF PRD RULE: POLICIES AND POLITICS

An Uneventful Election and a Mysterious Suicide

The elections of 1982 brought few surprises. Reluctantly, Guzmán honored his pledge not to seek reelection. The PRD nominated the party president, Senator Jorge Blanco (b. 1926), while the republic's most prominent septuagenarians, Balaguer and Bosch, ran at the head of their respective parties, the PR and the PLD. Jorge Blanco led with 46.7 percent of the vote. Balaguer followed with 39.2 percent, and Bosch trailed with 9.8 percent. Three minor candidates shared the remaining votes. The PRD won a majority of the Senate seats and a strong plurality in the Chamber of Deputies.[6]

Given the republic's troubled history, the orderliness of the election was in itself remarkable. Almost 90 percent of the 2.6 million eligible voters turned out, causing long lines at many of the 5611 polling stations and obliging election officials to keep polls open an extra 2 hours. Soldiers and police were posted at polling places, temporarily under the authority of the Central Election Board, but otherwise the security forces remained in their barracks. President-elect Jorge Blanco praised their professionalism, while the National Police command praised the electorate for "civilized and orderly" conduct.

The season's unpleasant surprise was to come 2 months after the election, when President Guzmán committed suicide. It was surmised that his reasons were personal, that he had been deeply shamed by the extent of corruption practiced by his daughter, Sonia, and apprehensive about public exposure of it.[7] His vice-president, Jacobo Majluta, assumed the presidency for the interim.

---

6. Julio Brea Franco, *El sistema constitucional dominicano*, Tomo II (Santo Domingo: Universidad Nacional Pedro Henríquez Ureña, 1983).
7. The suicide itself is the only firmly established fact of a far more complicated story. Though many political insiders are convinced that Guzmán himself was scrupulously honest, there is a broad consensus that Sonia is corrupt and unscrupulous and that she was highly influential in her father's government. Widely accredited rumors hold that Jorge Blanco informed Guzmán that Sonia's deals would have to be investigated, that Sonia, on her own or with Guzmán's agreement, attempted to provoke a coup in order to prlong her father's rule, and that Guzmán attempted to have Jorge Blanco or Peña Gómez or both assassinated. An incident that occurred shortly after the election, in which one of Sonia's bodyguards dropped and exploded a grenade in the parking lot of the JCE, is widely viewed as representing the abortion of a coup attempt; the grenade, it is believed, was to have been lobbed into the headquarters of the JCE.

The Rule of Jorge Blanco and the International Monetary Fund

Salvador Jorge Blanco, inaugurated in August 1982, had no considerable popular following of his own, but he brought to the presidency the reputation of a serious and honest lawyer—politician with a constructive program. He pledged to maintain and strengthen the social and political liberalism introduced by his predecessor; to stem the tide of corruption, to which the PRD itself had fallen prey; to trim the size of the bureaucracy, which had mushroomed under Guzmán; and to expand services and protections to the disadvantaged majority. Sadly, it has been in the nature of things—the urgency of majority needs, the scarcity of national resources, the extent of private greed, the omnipresence of military intimidation and U.S. guardianship, and the crushing pressures from foreign creditors—that Dominican presidents rarely leave office with their political stock intact. Economic and political circumstances largely beyond his control combined with the weaknesses of his own administration to make Jorge Blanco's presidency a troubled and disappointing one.

During his first few months in office, Jorge Blanco was able to launch a major new construction program to deal with the shortage of low-income housing, a program that, not coincidentally, was to employ some 50,000 workers. He also initiated a literacy program intended to reach some 400,000 adults. And he introduced new measures to stimulate agricultural production and to modernize industry. Many of the president's legislative proposals, however, were blocked in the Senate. The PRD finally had a majority there; but Majluta, who had been elected to the Senate in 1982 from the federal district, was building his own organization to run for the presidency in 1986, and he saw an obstructionist role as suiting his purposes.

Moreover, like Guzmán before him, Jorge Blanco was confronted with weak markets and sinking prices for the country's major exports, and thus with a growing balance-of-payments deficit. The current-accounts deficit combined with the requirements of servicing the foreign debt made austerity measures inescapable. In fact, the government's coffers were practically empty. Jorge Blanco sought first to tighten the belts of the more affluent, by banning entirely the importation of cars and more than a hundred other categories of goods designated luxuries; by raising taxes on other imports and on capital gains and real estate; by limiting the remission of dividends and slow-

8. THE NEW ERA OF PRD RULE: POLICIES AND POLITICS

ing capital flight; and by cutting the salaries of the top 5.6 percent in the public service. The president even cut his own salary by 40 percent.

The economic crisis, however, compelled him to appeal to the IMF for loans amounting to several hundred million dollars and to institute, in turn, the draconian measures demanded by that body. In October 1982 the government entered into a tentative agreement with the IMF on a 3-year credit package worth $467 million. For most Dominicans, the price was to be frozen wages, higher prices and interest rates, longer working hours, dwindling foreign-exchange reserves, and a spreading recession. By 1983, the three most important autonomous state agencies—the State Sugar Council, the Dominican Electricity Corporation, and the Dominican State Enterprises—were all close to bankruptcy.

Under the terms of the agreement, the government was forced to abandon most of its import restrictions, even on luxury items, and to ease export restrictions as well, diminishing the local food supply.[8] Through the introduction of a parallel market rate, via the commercial banks, the peso was steadily devalued. While the peso maintained its "official" parity to the dollar, on the parallel market it had sunk to about three to one by 1984. In February 1985 official parity was abandoned, and the parallel rate became official.

The deepening crisis also aggravated antagonisms among classes and sectors and seemed to leave civilian authorities more vulnerable to the machinations of the security forces. In the summer of 1983 the Departamento Nacional de Investigaciones (DNI) circulated a report that a guerrilla training school had been established. The report remained unsubstantiated, but the military nevertheless rounded up about 100 alleged leftists. Leaders of the Independent Peasant Movement were also arrested, as were 30 villagers from a remote rural area who had been agitating for the building of a local school.

The crisis also deepened the country's dependence on the United States. Before his own election to the presidency, Jorge Blanco had been highly critical of President Guzmán for his solicitation of foreign investment and his failure significantly to tighten local control over foreign businesses. Jorge Blanco's policies in that area, however, have not notably differed from those of his predecessor. In fact, his government formed a new committee to encourage foreign investment and

---

8. Rodríguez and Huntington, "Dominican Republic," p. 34.

introduced legislation designed to create a more favorable climate for such investment, including tax incentives to agro-exporters and measures to facilitate the repatriation of profits.

In January 1984, Jorge Blanco wrote to President Ronald Reagan, warning him that the terms exacted by the IMF might provoke social tensions so strong as to shatter the peace and undermine the democratic process in the Dominican Republic. Reagan dismissed the warning, but in April 1984, as the Dominican government began to implement another round of "adjustments" demanded by the IMF, the most serious civil strife the country had experienced since 1965 got under way.[9]

The immediate provocation was the government's announcement of a new round of price increases, as imported goods came to be subject to parallel-market exchange rates. The prices of all imported goods, including medicines, were to increase by 200 percent, and the lifting of government subsidies from many basic foodstuffs would mean higher prices, for example, for bread, flour, sugar, cooking oil, and condensed and powdered milk. Businessmen's organizations joined labor unions in declaring a 24-hour strike, and bands of youths barricaded streets with burning tires and threw rocks at police. The police responded with tear-gas grenades.

Demonstrations turned into riots, and stores were looted and burned. The riots that began in Santo Domingo spread within 3 days to more than 20 towns and cities. The government's response included closing down two radio stations and a television station and authorizing police occupation of union headquarters.

As the police proved unwilling to use the deadly force seen as necessary to put a stop to the riots, the government called in the so-called *Cazadores de la Montaña* (Highland Rangers), an elite unit trained by the U.S. military in counterinsurgency. They came in shooting real bullets. At least 100 protesters were killed.[10] Several hundred were wounded, and more than 4000 were arrested. In the aftermath of the riots, the United States offered some $50 million in new aid, and the IMF agreed to allow the republic to administer its medicines in smaller doses.

9. Tom Barry, Beth Wood, and Deb Preusch, *The Other Side of Paradise: Foreign Control in the Caribbean* (New York: Grove Press, 1984), pp. 291–292.
10. Human rights organizations documented the cases of 101 protesters killed by security forces. The government acknowledged only 55 casualties (Ramón Martínez, interview with the author).

8. THE NEW ERA OF PRD RULE: POLICIES AND POLITICS

The seriousness of the riots and of the reaction of the security forces had a sobering effect on the party system as it was gearing up for the next round of elections in 1986. Jorge Blanco had initially charged the PR with instigating the riots, but he subsequently toned down his rhetoric, and other government spokesmen followed suit. Opposition party leaders also began to exercise more caution and discretion, as all realized that further disturbances might result in military intervention and the early demise of their experiment in democracy.

The resourcefulness and statesmanship demanded by the seriousness of the economic crisis were not forthcoming, however, either from the government or from its congressional opposition. While the poorest Dominicans had no choice but to accept greater sacrifice, the affluent made the usual choice. Jorge Blanco's proposals for new taxes were blocked in Congress, not only by the *reformistas*, but by the PLD and the Majluta faction of the PRD as well.

In the absence of new resources, the most obvious means of reducing the budget deficit—as demanded by the IMF—would have been a pruning of public employees. Guzmán's approach to limiting unemployment and consolidating the base of the PRD had been expanding the government payroll. He did not fire the *reformistas* in government service, but added another layer of employees loyal to the PRD, increasing the number of employees by some 50 to 60 percent. Jorge Blanco had pledged to prune the bureaucracy, but he, too, found early on that such a move was not politically feasible. On the contrary, he found it necessary to expand the bureaucracy by another 40 percent or so. Whereas there had been about 120,000 government employees when the PRD assumed office in 1978, there were, by 1985, some 250,000.

Most government agencies, undercapitalized, stumbled along, performing their duties only sporadically. Some government programs maintained momentum, despite the scarcity of funds, but others were stopped in their tracks. Construction work on 6 major irrigation systems moved ahead, but the low-income housing project was abandoned in its naked foundations—a massive, instant ruin. The resettlement of peasant families on government land continued, but credit and technical support services were practically nonexistent. The Ministry of Agriculture did not have enough money to sustain strictly institutional maintenance operations—for example, paying its 13,000 employees—and then to fund rural support programs as well.[11]

11. Marion Ford, interview with the author.

Many of the government's proposals were farsighted and humane, but the budget crisis made mirth of them. The government had a bill before Congress, for example, to extend free health care to every Dominican.[12] Meanwhile, however, teachers were demonstrating because the health benefits already duly provided in their contracts were being denied them.

Among government agencies and programs, only the armed forces and police fared well—their budgets, for example, amounting to more than the combined budgets for health and education. It was because of the historic enmity between the PRD and the military, of course, rather than in spite of it, that military budgets, salaries, and perquisites were on the rise, while civilian programs floundered.

Upon assuming the presidency, Jorge Blanco moved quickly to retire high-ranking officers he considered "politicized." Both of the Imberts were retired in 1982. The position of secretary of state for the armed forces was assigned initially to General Matos González. He was moved in 1984 to the ministry of the interior and replaced by General Cuervo Gómez. Both Matos González and Cuervo Gómez were considered to be relatively apolitical and "professional." Most promotions were made on the basis of time in grade, and only 2 or 3 of the top 10 officers, along with 3 or 4 brigade commanders, were reportedly close to the president. Nevertheless, the officer corps balked at some of the president's nominees.[13]

It was most unlikely that the same Jorge Blanco who had represented thousands of Constitutionalist street fighters in negotiations with the military and the United States in 1965 had since become a great fan of the armed forces. Thus, his generosity toward them could only be seen as a whopping bribe to stay in their barracks and leave his government alone.

Apart from the armed forces and the PRD loyalists who had been able to get government jobs, just about the only Dominicans who had clearly benefited from the programs of the PRD-IMF government had been the bankers and other financiers engaged in currency-exchange operations. The expansion of imports and the opportunities for currency speculation provided by the parallel market had proved irresist-

---

12. Generoso Ramírez Morales, consultant on social security to the Organización Interamericano de Salud (regional arm of WHO), interview with the author, Santo Domingo, January 10, 1985.
13. Sources include Richard Hines and Wayne Wheeler, interviews with the author.

ible to moneymen, both in the government and in the private sector.[14]

It was generally believed that Jorge Blanco was personally honest, and that, unlike Balaguer, he had not intentionally used corruption as a tool of government. Nevertheless, even observers sympathetic to Jorge Blanco and the PRD were dismayed by the level of corruption in the mid 1980s. It appeared that many of the PRD appointees, previously poor, had been in a hurry to get rich, and that corruption had simply expanded in tandem with the expansion of the bureaucracy.

In early 1985 both inflation and unemployment were running higher than 30 percent by official calculations, and most believed that official figures greatly understated the problems. As the economic crisis deepened, the Congress dug in its collective heels, united in no purpose other than to block the president's budget. Jorge Blanco had no clear strategy for dealing either with the Congress or with the IMF. The government appeared to be drifting, immobilized by indecision and buffeted by forces beyond its control.

A new IMF accord, almost a year in the works, was reached in late January 1985. For most, it meant only more bad news. The announcement of price increases of 34 percent for gasoline and 20 to 60 percent for food was accompanied by the arrests of several hundred persons—particularly leftist and labor leaders—in four cities. Agitation continued, however. On February 11 a general strike, backed by 53 labor, business, and political organizations, was remarkably successful in closing down Santo Domingo and at least five other cities. The armed forces were mobilized, and several protestors were shot; and, once again, scores were arrested. Even Bosch was placed under house arrest. In the aftermath of the strike, Jorge Blanco announced a partial rollback in prices for basic food items.

Leaders of the PRD are appropriately concerned that the sinking economy may be taking with it their popular support and their hope for remaining in government. But they hope that the public—particularly the younger generation that has not known the risks the leaders assumed and the repression they endured—will appreciate what they have accomplished in the institutionalization of democracy, civil liberties, and civic order, and will appreciate as well that the new liberal order is fragile and may be lost.[15]

14. Among the several Dominicans who expressed this opinion were Ramón Martínez, Guido D'Alessandro, Joaquín Ricardo, and Damian Jiménez.
15. Winston Arnaud and Vincinte Sánchez, interviews with the author, Santo Domingo, January 10, 1985.

Ironically, in view of the fact that Jorge Blanco was known, above all, as a defender of human rights and civil liberties, the strongest criticism of the government in some quarters is that that liberal order is already being lost. The riots of April 1984 traumatized the government and the society and left civil liberties newly circumscribed. A new law of preventive detention allows the government to arrest and hold "suspects" for 48 hours without bringing charges against them. The device has been used liberally to round up "leftists" and labor leaders prior to the announcement of new price increases. Worse still, the security forces have seen it as a green light routinely to round up young people in the poorest neighborhoods, and political activists, at the university and elsewhere, are watched by the DNI.[16]

Abuses thus far have been in no way comparable to those experienced in Guatemala or Chile, for example, or even in Mexico. There have been no allegations of torture, as such, or of "disappearances," but the reappearance of political surveillance and arrests does not do honor to a government that prides itself on respect for citizens' rights. Moreover, as in the United States and elsewhere, the poor and otherwise defenseless are routinely mistreated by law enforcement and corrections officials, and the increase in political arrests has served to call attention to the more casual aspects of police brutality and inhumane prison conditions.[17]

Another source of concern in early 1985 was the appearance of an organization called the Movimiento Anti-Comunista Internacional (MACI). The acronym suddenly appeared, with ominous slogans, on walls all around Santo Domingo. A reliable source reported that MACI was being run by the DNI. The MACI operatives were military men, but they reported directly to the office of the president—specifically, to the president's chief of staff, Hatuey de Camps.

The MACI is multipurpose: It collects information, spreads propaganda, and intimidates. In general it generates fear, primarily on the

---

16. Teofílio Díaz, interview with the author.
17. Damian Jiménez says that the first time he and his PCD colleagues were detained, following the April 1984 riots, they were packed, along with nonpolitical detainees, into tiny cells, almost without light or air, in dreadfully unsanitary conditions. When they were released, they called a press conference to denounced prison conditions. The next time they were detained, it was in an office at the police station, away from prisons and nonpolitical prisoners.

8. THE NEW ERA OF PRD RULE: POLICIES AND POLITICS

left. It has also been used for specific purposes, such as to silence a deputy who was exposing corruption. It has not yet become a "death squad," but has recently brought a large supply of arms into the country.[18]

On the surface, the political system appears to be wide open and exuberantly free. But there are subtle means of containment and manipulation. The PCD, for example, has found itself unable to rent a radio transmitter. The DNI taps many telephones, including that of Peña Gómez.

The country's newspapers—about 10 dailies with a circulation of some 50,000—represent a broad range of views and appear to be assertive and critical, but the limits of their freedom are indicated by the stories they choose *not* to run. At the end of 1984, for example, many papers had neglected to run the usual *Resumen del Año* (loosely, "the Year in Review") because the top story would have had to be that of the April riots. (Editors have on occasion been subject to pressures from de Camps and from the military, but limits are basically self-imposed.)[19] Party leaders are busily gearing up for the campaign of 1986, but they often pull their punches. They know that some provocation—such as a new outbreak of rioting—might cause the fragile system to collapse.

The new democratic system has not brought with it the promised improvement in living standards. The masses of poor Dominicans have seen one source of hope after another bite the dust. Thus a polarization of sorts appeared to be developing between frightened businessmen and frustrated masses. Interestingly, however, that polarization was not being reflected in the attitudes of party leaders. On the contrary, it was deepening the cleavages within parties while drawing the ideological poles closer together.[20]

The explosiveness of the situation has caused unease among political leaders across the spectrum, and the example of turmoil in Central

---

18. The source, who is friendly with both de Camps and Jorge Blanco, does not believe that Jorge Blanco is aware of the operation. However, asked why he and others who know had not made a point of telling the president, he said that they could not be *sure* that he did not know already—that he was not behind it himself. The source believes that MACI is funded, directly or indirectly, by the CIA. De Camps, one of the three or four most powerful men in the country, also pays off several journalists with what the source believes to be CIA funds.
19. Ramón Martínez, interview with the author.
20. Julio Brea Franco, interview with the author, Santo Domingo, Januar 7, 1985.

America has had a sobering effect on both right and left. Party leaders on the left fear that rioting or other forms of civil disturbance on the part of the masses might lead to military intervention and violent repression. Civilian leaders on the right fear that military intervention and violent repression might lead to revolution. Furthermore, there is a generalized fear that the economic crisis is beyond solution, that under the restraints imposed by the IMF not even the most honest, competent, and committed government could bring relief. And no party wants to bear alone the blame for the hardships that are seen as inevitable. Thus, the suggestion of a co-government between the major parties has come from several quarters and is being treated seriously. Balaguer, for example, proposed to Peña Gómez that they consider the establishment of a broad-front government headed by a widely respected nonpartisan figure. Peña Gómez was reportedly receptive to the idea. The name of Rafael Herrera, editor of *Listín Diario*, was floated until Hererra expressed lack of interest.

The co-government concept has many critics in the major parties as well as in minor ones. Vincho Castillo of the FNP, for example, contends that such a co-government, in power, would simply become the pole on the right, thus strengthening the more radical left and increasing rather than mitigating polarization. Balaguer's nephew, Joaquín Ricardo, sees possibilities in a government in which all sectors are represented, but he would not call on an apolitical figure to head it. "The apolitical," he says, "are sharks." It seems unlikely that a co-government accord will actually be reached; but the fact that it has struck a responsive chord in many leaders and is being seriously discussed testifies to the depth of concern over the economic crisis and to the sophistication of the political elite.

9
CONCLUSION

Passing the Mantle

"What hope is there for the country?" *Listín Diario* once mused editorially. "One of our caudillos must hear everything and the other must say everything!" The two caudillos, Balaguer and Bosch, have in many ways symbolized the debilitating heritage of the Trujillo era. Both are brilliant scholars; both, in their fashions, are populists; and both were rendered ineffective as national leaders by Trujillo: Balaguer by being too close, Bosch by being too remote. Balaguer the extrovert was rendered an introvert, then coopted and tainted by his association with Trujillo and his thugs. Bosch the idealist, too long in exile, was unable to gain his footing in the grisly reality of Dominican politics. Until Bosch turned away from the mass party he had founded, the two caudillos also symbolized the basic cleavage in the Dominican polity, a cleavage based less on class than on traditional versus modern and rural versus urban orientations.

Defying the odds of time and fortune, the caudillos remained very prominently on the scene in 1985 and continued to command the political loyalty of a great many Dominicans. Nevertheless, as a practical matter, the mantle of leadership had passed to another generation. This generation came of age with the death of Trujillo. The popular uprising and U.S. intervention of 1965 represented at once its finest hour and its saddest. During the subsequent long reign of Balaguer, virtually all political activists, including some now aligned with him, suffered death threats, narrow escapes, detainment, and deportation. They learned both to accept risk and to exercise caution. PRD president

Vicente Sánchez, arrested 23 times during the presidency of Balaguer, marvels at the naiveté of today's youth, who seem to take freedom for granted.

The most able and most resilient politician of this post-Trujillo generation, Peña Gómez, now faces his moment of truth. The only PRD leader with a mass following, he has been viewed as a dangerous adversary by many in the business community, the military, and the U.S. government. Consequently, he has bided his time, promoting less popular party colleagues. It is not clear that his enemies have mellowed or that even the wisest and most committed leader could spring the country from the net thrown by the IMF. But the times demand leadership. If he does not rise to it now, he may find later his base has dissolved.

A Family Affair

Guido D'Alessandro is a founder and lifelong leader of the Social Christian party. As a very young man, he joined the clandestine Fourteenth of June movement, led by his uncle, Manuel Tavares Justo, a prominent Communist, to struggle against Trujillo. He joined the movement because, in the company of his brother-in-law, Ramfis Trujillo, he had been exposed to the horrors of Trujillismo. (Ramfis took his revenge by having D'Alessandro's younger brother murdered.) Soon after the founding of their party in 1961, the Social Christians withdrew from the Fourteenth of June movement because, unlike the movement's Communist contingent, they were unwilling to accept guidance from the CIA.[1]

The Social Christians were closely allied with the PRD in the 1960s, moved toward nonalignment in the 1970s, and in the 1980s merged with Balaguer's *Reformistas* to form the new PRSC. Meanwhile, D'Alessandro had served as the Balaguer government's ambassador to Venezuela and as its minister of industry and commerce. He maintained his links to the PRD, however. In fact, he was a close friend of

---

1. D'Alessandro says that he worked with other Social Christians and with Communists in the Fourteenth of June movement in the preparation of radio programs, underwritten by the CIA and broadcast from Swan Island, for a Dominican audience. He quit the project when the CIA tried to censor his programs. He says that the Social Christians left the Fourteenth of June movement in part because, unlike the Communists, they objected to working with the CIA.

9. CONCLUSION

Peña Gómez, having shared with him a night of terror in 1974, when Peña Gómez was seeking refuge from would-be military assassins.

D'Alessandro is an extraordinarily able politician, but the breadth of his political connections is not unusual in the small world of the Dominican political elite. Figuratively, and to a large extent literally as well, Dominican politics is a family affair. Virtually every political leader or group has been at one time allied with, and at another in conflict with, every other leader or group. Almost every political leader was at one time a guerrilla or conspirator against established authority, and every guerrilla has had a cousin who was a military officer or a banker.

Such factors as class conflict, ideology, and program, caudillismo and charisma, even personal interest and ambition only partially explain the dynamics of Dominican politics. Some curious twists in the political drama can be understood only with reference to family ties or family enmities, to shared experiences of danger, triumph, or defeat, or to episodes of mutual assistance or betrayal.

Were ideology to govern, one might expect that the bitterest rivalries would be found between Balaguer and Bosch or Balaguer and Peña Gómez. In fact, one finds a surprising level of mutual respect between Balaguer and Bosch and an inclination to accommodation between Balaguer and Peña Gómez. The bitterest political rivalry in the mid 1980s was between Peña Gómez and Bosch. They were competing, of course, for the same political constituency; but associates of the two men claimed that the "bad blood" between them was more personal than political. Like estranged spouses, they shared too many secrets.

The Best of Times, The Worst of Times

One who knew the Dominican Republic of the Trujillo era—one who has know the face of tyranny—has only to see the faces of young Dominicans—open, expressive, assertive—to sense the extent of political change the country has experienced. On most days, at least, the game of politics seems almost a celebration of freedom.

Nor has political freedom unleashed the anarchy of unorganized violent crime so common in the United States and elsewhere. Apart from crimes perpetrated by the police, assaults, muggings, and armed robbery are most rare. Teenagers stand around on street corners until all hours of the night holding great wads of pesos to change (illegally) for dollars with no apparent fear of being robbed.

Nevertheless, every house or business establishment of the least pretension has its own private armed guard. Private guard services constitute a lucrative business for retired generals and for the society a means of disguising unemployment. But they also constitute a recognition that a conspicuous few have gotten too rich too fast at the expense of too many.

Political freedom has yet to find expression in economic opportunity, except for those adept at graft. In fact, the opening of the political system has coincided with a virtual closing of the economic one. For reasons beyond the competency of political leaders, the country is experiencing its worst economic crisis in half a century.

It would be hard to overestimate the problems and challenges facing the Dominican government in the mid 1980s—in particular, the obstacles to economic development posed by the shrinking market for sugar, the rising foreign debt, and the currency devaluations imposed by the IMF. The good intentions, and in many cases good legislation, of the PRD have been virtually nullified by the lack of funds for implementation.

The PRD presents itself as the only truly modern political party, the one responsible for the institutionalization of democratic government, of law and order and respect for human rights and civil liberties, and the only party capable of maintaining that standard. Its opponents of both right and left, however, note that governmental abuses of rights and liberties have increased markedly since the riots of April 1984, and they charge that far from curtailing corruption, the PRD has merely multiplied the number of hands illicitly in the till.

Nevertheless, the PRD's political adversaries can take scant comfort in the government's political and economic failures. Those failures point up the dilemma that, in the explosive political climate of the mid 1980s, any Dominican government must face. If it reaches out beyond the parameters drawn by the IMF, the United States, certain business interests, and the armed forces to respond to the urgent needs of the poor majority, it runs the risk of being overthrown. If it *fails* to reach out and respond to majority needs, it runs the risk, at best, of losing its political following, at worst, of confronting massive insurrection.

BIBLIOGRAPHY

Books

Alum, Rolando, Jr. "Dominican Republic," pages 266–274 in George E. Delury (ed.), *World Encyclopedia of Political Systems and Parties*, Vol. 1. New York: Facts on File, 1983.

Atkins, G. Pope. *Arms and Politics in the Dominican Republic*. Boulder, CO: Westview Press, 1981.

Atkins, G. Pope, and Larman C. Wilson. *The United States and the Trujillo Regime*. New Brunswick, NJ: Rutgers University Press, 1972.

Barry, Tom, Beth Wood, and Deb Preusch. *The Other Side of Paradise: Foreign Control in the Caribbean*. New York: Grove Press, 1984.

Bell, Ian. *The Dominican Republic*. Boulder, CO: Westview Press, 1981.

Berrios Martínez, Ruben. "Dependent Capitalism and the Prospects for Democracy in Puerto Rico and the Dominican Republic," pages 327–339 in Paget Henry and Carl Stone (eds.), *The Newer Caribbean: Decolonization, Democracy and Development*. Philadelphia: Institute for the Study of Human Issues, 1983.

Bosch, Juan. *Composición social dominicana: história e interpretación*. Santo Domingo: Editora Alfa y Omega, 1981.

Bosch, Juan. *The Unfinished Experiment: Democracy in the Dominican Republic*. New York: Praeger, 1965.

Brea Franco, Julio. *El sistema constitucional domincano*, Vols. 1 and 2. Santo Domingo: Universidad Nacional Pedro Henríquez Ureña, 1983.

Calder, Bruce J. *The Impact of Intervention: The Dominican Republic during the U.S. Occupation of 1916–1924*. Austin: University of Texas Press, 1984.

Chomsky, Noam, and Edward S. Herman. *The Washington Connection and Third World Fascism*. The Political Economy of Human Rights, Vol. 1. Boston: South End Press, 1979.

Corkran, Herbert, Jr. *Patterns of International Cooperation in the Caribbean 1942−1969*. Dallas: Southern Methodist University Press, 1970.

Crassweller, Robert D. *The Caribbean Community: Changing Societies and U.S. Policy*. New York: Praeger, 1972.

Crassweller, Robert D. *Trujillo, the Life and Times of a Caribbean Dictator*. New York: Macmillan, 1966.

Diederich, Bernard. *Trujillo: The Death of the Goat*. Boston: Little, Brown, 1978.

Duarte, Isis. *Capitalismo y superpoblación en Santo Domingo; mercado de trabajo rural y ejército de reserva urbano*. Santo Domingo: CODIA, 1980.

Fagg, John Edwin. *Cuba, Haiti, and the Dominican Republic*. The Modern Nations in Historical Perspective Series. Englewood Cliffs, NJ: Prentice-Hall, 1965.

Fauriol, Georges A. "The Dominican Republic and Haiti: The Limitations of Foreign Policies," pages 182−192 in Richard Millett and W. Marvin Will (eds.), *The Restless Caribbean: Changing Patterns of International Relations*. New York: Praeger, 1979.

Forum (Rafael Herrera, president). *Los Problemas de la institutcionalización y preservación de la democrácia en la República Domincana*. Santo Domingo: Editora Alfa y Omega, 1977.

Free, Lloyd A. *Attitudes, Hopes and Fears of the Dominican People*. Princeton, NJ: Institute for International Social Research, 1965.

Gleijeses, Piero. *The Dominican Crisis*. Baltimore: Johns Hopkins University Press, 1978.

Goff, Fred, and Michael Locker. "The Politics of Interventionism: The U.S. in the Dominican Republic," pages 263−294 in Eric R. Wolf and Edward C. Hansen (eds.), *The Human Condition in Latin America*. New York: Oxford University Press, 1972.

Goodwin, Paul B., Jr. (ed.). *Global Studies: Latin America*. Guilford, CT: Dushkin Publishing Group, 1984.

Gutiérrez, Carlos María. *The Dominican Republic: Rebellion and Repression* (trans. Richard E. Edwards). New York: Monthly Review Press, 1972.

Herman, Edward S., and Frank Brodhead. *Demonstration Elections: U.S.-Staged Elections in the Dominican Republic, Vietnam, and El Salvador*. Boston: South End Press, 1984.

Horowitz, Michael M. *Peoples and Cultures of the Caribbean: An Anthropological Reader*. New York: Natural History Press, 1971.

Institute for the Comparative Study of Political Systems. *Dominican Republic Election Factbook, June 1, 1966*. Washington, DC: Institute for the Comparative Study of Political Systems (ICOPS), 1966.

Lemoine, Maurice. *Azucar Amargo: hay esclavos en el Caribe*. Santo Domingo: Ediciones CEPAE, 1983.

Logan, Rayford W. *Haiti and the Dominican Republic*. New York: Oxford University Press, 1968.

Lowenthall, Abraham F. *The Dominican Intervention*. Cambridge, MA: Harvard University Press, 1972.

Martin, John Bartlow. *Overtaken by Events: The Dominican Crisis from the Fall of Trujillo to the Civil War*. New York: Doubleday, 1966.

Martínez, Pablo A. *Resistencia campesina, imperialismo y reforma agraria en República Dominicana (1899–1978)*. Santo Domingo: Ediciones CEPAE, 1984.

Mashek, Robert W., and Stephen G. Vetter. *La Fundación Interamericana en la República Dominicana: Una década de apoyo a las organizaciones de desarrollo locales*. Rosslyn, VA: Fundación Interamericana, 1983.

Moreno, Jose A. *Barrio in Arms: Revolution in Santo Domingo*. Pittsburgh: University of Pittsburgh Press, 1970.

Pattee, Ricardo. *La República Dominicana*. Madrid: Ediciones Cultura Hispanica, 1967.

República Domincana en Cifras, V. Santo Domingo: Secretário Técnico de la Presidéncia, December 1970.

Rodman, Seldon. *Quisqueya: A History of the Dominican Republic*. Seattle: University of Washington Press, 1964.

Santana, Osvaldo. *Peña Gómez: sus origenes*. Santo Domingo: Editora El Nuevo Diario, 1981.

Santana, Santiago. *Actualidad y perspectivas de la economía dominicana, 1970–1980*. Santo Domingo: Editora Alfa y Omego, 1977.

Serulle Ramia, José, and Jacqueline Boin. *La inversión de capitalies imperialistas en la República Domincana*. Santo Domingo: Ediciones Gramil, 1981.

Slater, Jerome. *Intervention and Negotiation: The United States and the Dominican Republic*. New York: Harper & Row, 1970.

Wiarda, Howard J. *The Dominican Republic: Nation in Transition*. New York: Praeger, 1968.

Wiarda, Howard J., and Michael J. Kryzanek. *The Dominican Republic: A Caribbean Crucible*. Boulder, CO: Westview Press, 1982.

Weil, Thomas E., et al. *Area Handbook for the Dominican Republic*. Washington, DC: Government Printing Office, 1973.

Williams, Eric. *From Columbus to Castro: The History of the Caribbean 1492–1969*. New York: Harper & Row, 1970.

Wipfler, William L. *The Churches of the Dominican Republic in the Light of History*. Cuernavaca, Mexico: Centro Intercultural de Documentacion, 1966.

Periodicals

Dorsey, Jeff, Sheldon Annis, and Stephen Vetter. "Credit to Small Farmers in the Dominican Republic: Beyond Revolving Loan Funds." *Grassroots Development*, 6, No. 2, and Vol. 7, No. 1, 1983, pp. 19–26.

Draper, Theodore. "The Dominican Intervention Reconsidered." *Political Science Quarterly*, Vol. 86, No. 1, March 1971, pp. 1–36.

Gardiner, C. Harvey. "The Japanese and the Dominican Republic." *Inter-American Economic Affairs* (Washington, DC), Vol. 25, No. 3, Winter 1971, pp. 23–38.
Goodsell, James Nelson. "Balaguer's Dominican Republic." *Current History*, Vol. 53, No. 315, November 1967, pp. 298–302.
Moya Pons, Frank. "La Política Domincana: Agosto 1984." *LASA Forum*, Vol. 15, No. 3, Fall 1984, pp. 19–21.
Rodríguez, Adrian, and Deborah Huntington. "Dominican Republic—the Launching of a Democracy." *NACLA Report on the Americas*, Vol. 16, No. 6, November–December 1982, pp. 2–35.
Vetter, Stephen. "Portrait of a Peasant Leader: Ramón Aybar." *Grassroots Development*, Vol. 8, No. 1, 1984, pp. 2–11.
Walker, Malcolm T. "Power Structure and Patronage in a Community of the Dominican Republic." *Journal of Inter-American Studies and World Affairs* (Coral Gables, FL), Vol. 12, No. 4, October, 1970, pp. 485–504.
Wedge, Bryant. "The Case Study of Student Political Violence: Brazil, 1964, and the Dominican Republic, 1965." *World Politics* (Princeton, NJ), Vol. 21, No. 2, January 1969, pp. 183–206.
Wiarda, Howard J. "The Development of the Labor Movement in the Dominican Republic." *Inter-American Economic Affairs*, (Washington, DC), Vol. 20, No. 1, Summer 1966, pp. 41–63.

Newspapers (November 1982–January 1985)

Camino, semanario Catolico nacional, Santiago de los Caballeros.
Diario Las Américas, Miami.
El Caríbe, Santo Domingo.
Listín Diario, Santo Domingo.
El Nacional de 'Ahora!, Santo Domingo.
New York Times.
Santo Domingo News.
Temas del Tiempo, gobierno de concentracion nacional, Santo Domingo.
Wall Street Journal.
Ya, Santiago de los Caballeros.

Party Organs

Hablan los comunistas (PCD).
Tribuna Democrática (PRD).
Vanguardia del Pueblo (PLD).

Other Sources

Banco Central de la República Dominicana, Santo Domingo. *Boletín Mensual*, Vol. 36, No. 7, July 1982.
Banco Central de la República Domincana, Departamento de Estudios Económicos, *Cuentas Nacionales: Producto Nacional Bruto 1974–1978*. Santo Domingo, 1980.
Constitution of the Dominican Republic 1966. Washington, DC: Pan American Union, Organization of American States, General Secretariat, 1967.
Espinal, Fulgencio. *Breve história del PRD*. Santo Domingo: Ediciones Tercer Mundo, March 1980.
Fondo de Inversiones para el Desarrollo Económico (FIDE). *Informe Trimestral, Octúbre–Diciembre, 1981*. Santo Domingo: Banco Central de la República Dominicana.
Jorge Blanco, Salvador (president 1982–1986). *Programa de Gobierno*. Santo Domingo: Gobierno de Concentracion Nacional, 1982.
Servicio de Documentación CEDEE. *Notas para el análisis del movimiento obrero en República Dominicana en 1983*. Santo Domingo: CEDEE, 1984.
U.S. Agency for International Development. *United States Overseas Loans and Grants and Assistance from International Organizations Obligations and Loan Authorizations, July 1, 1945–June 30, 1971*. Washington, DC: Government Printing Office, May 24, 1972.
U.S. Department of State, Bureau of Public Affairs. *Atlas of the Caribbean Basin*, 2d ed. Washington, DC: Government Printing Office, July 1984.
U.S. Embassy, Santo Domingo. *The Dominican Republic: Investment Climate Report*. December 1984.
U.S. Embassy, Santo Domingo. *Foreign Economic Trends and Their Implications for the United States: The Dominican Republic*. July 1984.

Interviews

Santo Domingo, Dominican Republic, unless otherwise indicated, November 1982 and January 1985:

J. Winston Arnaud G., Acting Secretary-General, Partido Revolucionario Domincano (PRD), January 10.
Bob Brown, Staff Member, Office of the U.S. Military Attaché, U.S. Embassy, January 8.
First Lieutenant Claudio Caamaño, nephew of Colonel Francisco Caamaño Deñó and survivor of guerrilla invasion of February 1973, January 14.
Marino Vinicio ("Vincho") Castillo, lawyer and president of the National Executive Directorate of the Fuerza Nacional Progresista (FNP); former member of Congress (1961), minister of labor, and adviser to the Balaguer government on land reform legislation, January 4.

Guido D'Alessandro, businessman; founding member of Partido Revolucionario Social Christiano (PRSC); ambassador to Venezuela and minister of commerce and industry under government of President Balaguer; member of Congress 1978–1982. January 4, Boca Chica; January 13, Santo Domingo.

Teofílio Díaz, director of projects, Centro de Planificación y Acción Ecuménica (CEPAE), January 8.

Percy Duran, Peace Corps director for the Dominican Republic, November 1982.

Euclides Gutiérrez Félix, public information officer, Partido de Liberación Dominicana (PLD). January 5.

Marion Ford, agriculture officer, U.S. Agency for International Development. January 8.

Julio Brea Franco, dean of the College of Social Sciences, Technological Institute of Santo Domingo, January 7.

José Francisco Peña Gómez, mayor of Santo Domingo and secretary-general of the PRD. January 11.

James M. Hawley III, economic counselor, U.S. Embassy, January 8.

Richard Hines, political counselor, U.S. Embassy, January 3.

Bishop Telésforo A. Isaac, head of the Dominican Anglican Episcopal church, January 12, Puerto Plata.

Damian Jiménez, member of the executive council, Partido Comunista Dominicana (PCD), January 10.

Joe Joyner, staff member, Office of the U.S. Military Attaché, U.S. Embassy, January 2.

Félix Koch, member of Jewish refugee community resettled in Sosua, on the north coast of the Dominican Republic, in 1940, January 12, Sosua.

Ramón B. Martínez-Portorreal, lawyer, professor of law, and executive secretary of the Dominican Committee on Human Rights, November 1982 and January 7, 1985.

Alfonso Moreno Martínez, businessman; founding member and former presidential candidate of the Partido Revolucionario Social Cristiano (PRSC), November 1982 and January 2 and 10, 1985.

Generoso Ramírez Morales, Consultant on social security to the Organización Interamericano de Salud (regional arm of the World Health Organization), January 10.

Rafael Moya, minister of labor under the government of President Guzmán November 1982.

Joaquín A. Ricardo, secretary-general of the Partido Reformista Social Christiano (PRSC) and nephew of Joaquín Balaguer, January 10.

Yvette Sabbagh, sociologist, Centro de Estudios de la Realidad Social Dominicana (CERESD), Universidad Autónoma de Santo Domingo (UASD), January 7.

Vicente Sánchez, president, Partido Revolucionario Dominicana (PRD), January 10.
Eduardo Súarez, commercial officer, U.S. Embassy, January 2.
Wellone Modeste Valerio, speical assistant to José Francisco Peña Gómez, January 10 and 11.
Carlos Villaverde, director, Centro Dominicano de Estudios de la Educación (CEDEE), January 8.
Sacha Z. Volman, consultant to the Dominican government on labor affairs; formerly director of the Centro Interamericano de Estudios Sociales (CIDES), adviser to President Bosch and to President Kennedy, having access to CIA funds, January 14.
Colonel Wayne Wheeler, U.S. military attaché, U.S. Embassy, January 8.

INDEX

Agreement of Malpasse, 120
Agriculture
   dependency on, 62–64
   economic growth and, 62–64
AIFLD (American Institute for Free Labor Development), 35, 95–96, 117
Alcázar de Colón, 6, 16
Alianza Social Demócrata (ASD), 89
Alliance for Progress, 43, 117
Altos de Chavon, 9
Alvarez Boegart, Fernando, 86
American Institute for Free Labor Development (AIFLD), 35, 95–96, 117
Amiama Tío, Luis, 29, 34
Angel Ramírez, Miguel, 38
Arias, Desiderio, 21
Armed forces, 102–107
   under Balaguer, 103–105
   under Guzmán, 105–106, 130–132
   under Jorge Blanco, 142
   social class and, 57–58
   under Trujillo, 102–103, 119
Armed Forces Education Center (CEFA), 34
Audiencia, 16, 17
Augusto Lora, Francisco, 46, 47
Autonomous Confederation of Christian Unions (CASC), 86, 95–96, 97–98
Autonomous University of Santo Domingo (UASD), 90, 101–102
Aybar, Ramón, 71, 72

Báez, Buenaventura, 19, 20
Balaguer, Joaquín, 29, 30, 34, 36, 40–54, 69, 76, 78, 79, 85, 86, 90, 116, 135, 147, 149
   armed forces and, 103–105
   Catholic Church and, 100
   changes made by, 43–44
   characteristics of, 42–43
   civil violence under, 48–49

   corruption under, 44–45, 67, 76, 104
   election of 1966 and, 40–42, 121
   election of 1970 and, 46–47
   election of 1974 and, 49–51
   election of 1978 and, 52–54, 115
   Haiti and, 121
   land reform under, 60
   new elites under, 57
   organized labor and, 96–97
   relation with Latin America, 124, 125
   student groups and, 101–102
Banda, La (The Band), 48–49
Baseball, 23
Bauxite, 64
Beauchamp Javier, Juan René, 52, 130
Bétancourt, Rómulo, 28, 32, 112, 124, 128
Blacks, 57–58
   as slaves, 15–18
Bloque Socialista (BS), 89
Blue party, 20
Bluhdorn, Charles, 68
Bolívar, Simón, 18
Bonnelly, Rafael F., 40
Bosch, Juan, 31–39, 40, 41–42, 45, 47, 48, 50, 51, 120
   Catholic Church and, 99
   Dominican Liberation Party and, 87–88
   Haiti and, 120–121
   land reform under, 60
   Organization of American States (OAS) and, 127
   organized labor and, 95–96
   relations with Europe, 126
   relations with Latin America, 124, 125
Boyer, Jean-Pierre, 18
Brandt, Willy, 123

Caamaño Deñó, Francisco, 34, 38, 46, 50, 103
Caamaño Grullón, Claudio, 50

Cabral, Donald Reid, 85, 103
Cabrera, Mario, 94
Cáceres, Ramón, 20
Caribbean Coastal Plain, 4-6
Caribbean Community, 128
Caribbean Legion, 32
Caribs, 14
Cartagena group, 126
Carter, Jimmy, 8, 52, 53, 115
Casa de Campo complex, 6, 9
Casas, Bartolomé de las, 15
CASC (Autonomous Confederation of Christian Unions), 86, 95-96, 97-98
Castro, Fidel, 112, 125
Catholic Church, 27, 40, 98-101
Cazadores de la Montaña (Highland Rangers), 140
Central American Common Market, 128
Central Election Board (JCE), 80
Central Intelligence Agency (CIA), 28, 33, 34
Chile, 144
Christian Democratic Confederación Latinoamericano Sindical (CLAS), 98
Christianity, 15
Christian Revolutionary University Group (BRUC), 101
Cibao Valley, 4, 14
Cline, Ray, 41
Colombia, 22
Colonial period, 6, 7-8
 France and, 17-18
 Spanish occupation in, 14-17
Columbus, Bartolomeo, 15
Columbus, Christopher, 6, 13-15, 16
Columbus, Diego, 16
Communal lands, 23, 44
Communism, 33-34, 37, 38-39, 52, 88, 89, 117, 122
CONATRAL (National Federation of Free Laborers), 35, 95-96, 117
Concepción de la Vega, 17
Confederation of Organized Labor (COSTO), 96-97
Congress, 77
Constabulary force, 23-24, 25
Constitution, 31, 43
Constitutionalists, 38-39, 42, 46, 59, 96, 99, 103, 117-118, 128
Costa Rica, 32
Crime, 48-149
Cruz Brea, José Ernesto, 106
Cuba, 22, 28, 56, 112, 115, 118, 120, 125, 127
Cuervo Gómez, Manuel Antonion, 106, 142
Culture, 6-7
Customs agreement of 1905, 21, 111, 116

D'Alessandro, Guido, 87, 148-149
Davis, Martin S., 68
Debt, 21, 110-111

Democratic Socialist University Front (FUSD), 101
Department of National Investigation (DNI), 105, 139, 145
Dependency, on sugar, 62-63
Dessalines, Jean Jacques, 18
Development, 1-3, 10-12
 in the "Dominican miracle" of 1970, 43-44
 foreign enterprises and, 70
 goals of, 10-11
 lower classes and, 59
 political setting and, 11, 12
 problems of, 11-12
Diet, 58
Dominican Agrarian Institute, 60
Dominican Church, 98-101
Dominican Communist party (PCD), 37, 52, 88, 89
Dominican Liberation party (PLD), 51, 87-89
Dominican Popular Movement (MPD), 37
Dominican Revolutionary party (PRD), 11, 31, 37, 40, 42, 45-48, 49, 59, 81-84, 117, 150. *See also* Guzmán, Antonio
 election of 1974 and, 49-51, 53-54
 election of 1978 and, 52-54
 under Jorge Blanco, 138
 organized labor and, 95-97
Drake, Francis, 17
Duarte, Juan Pablo, 19
Duvalier, Francois, 120, 121
Duvalier, Jean Claude, 122

Economic growth, 62-73
 foreign investment and, 66-70
 history of, 62-65
 Rivera de Payabo region and, 70-73
Eisenhower, Dwight, 28
Electoral system, 80-81
Elite classes, 56-57, 93-94
Encomienda, 16
Enrique (Taino leader), 14-15
Enriquillo (Jesus Galván), 15
Estrella Ureña, Rafael, 25
Europe, 126
Executive branch, 75-77

Falconbridge, 66, 69
Families, marriage and, 62
Fanjul brothers, 6, 68-69
Federal Bureau of Investigation (FBI), 33
Federation of Dominican Students (FED), 101, 102
Federation of Peasant Brotherhoods (FENHERCA), 33
Fernández, Eduardo, 135
Fiallo, Viriato, 31
Figueres, José, 32, 124
Foreign policy, 109-128
 domestic correlates of, 110-112
 expansion of, 122-128

INDEX

with Haiti, 110, 119–122
with the United States, 111–119
Fourteenth of June movement, 36, 37, 148
Fragua, 101
France
  cession of Haiti to, 7–8
  colonial period, 17–18
  slave revolt of 1791 and, 17–18
Franchise, 80
Franciso Tavares, Rafael, 89
Frente Izquerdista Dominicana (FID), 89
Fuerza Nacional Progresista (FNP), 90

Galíndez, Jesús María de, 27
Galo Plaza, 52, 127
García Godoy, Héctor, 39–40, 42, 47
General Confederation of Labor (CGT), 90, 97
General Union of Dominican Workers (UGTD), 97
Germany, 114, 119
Gold, 11, 64
  Spanish conquest and, 13–14, 16
Government, 75–81. *See also* Political parties
  electoral system, 80–81
  executive branch, 75–77. *See also* specific presidents
  Gulf and Western Corporation and, 9–10, 67
  judiciary, 78–79
  legislative branch, 77–78
  provincial and local, 79–80
Government employees, 141–142
Grant, Ulysses S., 8
Gross domestic product (GDP), 64
Guardia Nacional Dominicana (Dominican National Guard), 24
Guardia Republicana, 24
Guatemala, 120, 144
Guayacanes, 6
Gulf and Western Corporation, 6, 67–69, 135
  government and, 9–10, 67
  influence of, 8–10
  unloading of property by, 6, 10, 68–69
Guzmán, Antonio, 51, 54, 63, 76, 78, 82, 83, 129–137
  armed forces and, 105–106, 130–132
  challenging of party regulars by, 134–35
  economic decline and, 132–134
  election of 1982, 137
  Haiti and, 122
  relation with Latin America, 124, 125
  suicide of, 137
  tourism and, 64–65
  United States and, 135–136

Haiti, 1, 3, 22, 132
  cession to France, 7–8
  laborers from, 60, 61–62, 68, 119, 121–122
  massacre of 1937 and, 119
  occupation by, 18–19, 110
  of the Taino people, 13–14
Henríquez y Carvajal, Francisco, 21–22
Hérard, Charles, 19
Herbicides, 72
Herrera, Rafael, 146
Heureaux, Ulises, 20, 110
Hispaniola
  cession to France by Spain, 7–8
  described, 1–3
  indigenous population of, 13–15
History of the Indies (Casas), 15
Hoover, J. Edgar, 33
Hurricanes, 133–134, 136

IAPF (Inter-American Peace Force), 39, 42, 45, 127
Imbert Barrera, Antonio, 29, 34, 136
Imbert McGregor, Alfredo Segundo, 136
Imbert McGregor, Mario Alfredo, 136
Impeachment, 78
Independence day, 19
Independent Democratic Action (ADI), 93
Independent Peasant Movement (MCI), 98, 139
Industrialization, 69–70
Inflation, 65, 76, 132, 143
Institute for Political Education, 32
Institutional Act, 103
Insurgency, 24–25
Inter-American Center for Social Studies (CIDES), 33, 34
Inter-American Development Bank, 128
Inter-American Foundation, 72
Inter-American Peace Force (IAPF), 39, 42, 45, 127
Inter-American Treaty of Reciprocal Assistance (Rio Treaty), 120
Interest groups, 93–107
  armed forces, 102–107. *See also* Armed forces
  Catholic Church, 27, 40, 98–101
  economic elite, 56–57, 93–94
  organized labor, 95–98
  peasant movements, 98
  students, 101–102
International Monetary Fund (IMF), 11, 65, 118, 128, 139, 140, 143, 146
Isabela (settlement), 14, 15
Isidro Jiménez, Juan, 21

Jesus Galván, Manuel de, 15
Jesús López Rodríguez, Nicolás de, 100
Jiminéz Reyes, Ramón Emilio, 131

Joaquín Castillo, Manuel, 53
Johnson, Lyndon B., 36, 38, 41, 43, 114, 115, 117–118
Jorge Blanco, Salvador, 65, 76–77, 82, 83, 106, 124, 125–126, 138–146
   corruption under, 143–144
   economic problems, 138–140, 142–143
   government employees under, 141–142
   United States and, 139–140
Judiciary, 78–79

Kennedy, John F., 32–36, 115, 116, 117

Labor Front for Union Autonomy—Labor Center for Dominican Workers (FOUPSA—CESITRADO), 95–96
Labor groups, 95–98
La Estructura (The Structure), 83
Lajara Burgos, 46–47
Land
   communal, 23, 44
   encomienda and, 16
   poverty and, 59, 60
   redistribution of, 31, 44, 60
   repartimiento and, 16
Land registration act, 23
Lansing, Robert, 21
La Romana, 6, 67, 69
Latin America, 123, 124, 125. *See also* specific countries
Latin American Free Trade Association, 128
Legislature, 77–78
Literature, 6
Lluberes Montas, Salvador, 130
Local government, 79–80
Long, Fritz, 35
Lower class, 58–61, 144, 145
Loyalists, 38–39
Luperon, Gregorio, 20

Majluta, Jacobo, 76, 82, 83, 84, 137, 138, 141
Majoritarian CGT (PGT Mayoritaria), 97
Marriage, 62
Marte Pichardo, Melido, 105
Martin, John Bartlow, 33, 35, 38
Matos González, Ramiro, 107, 142
Mella, Ramón, 19
Mendes, Hector, 107
Mexico, 144
Middle class, 57–58
Migration of population, 61–62
Military. *See* Armed forces
Minifundios, 59
Minimum-wage rate, 133
Mining, 1, 64
Molina Ureña, José Rafael, 36, 37, 38

Monroe Doctrine, 113
Montes Arache, Manuel, 38
Morales Troncoso, Carlos, A., 21, 69
Moreno Martinez, Alfonso, 47
Movement for Democratic Integration against Reelection (MIDA), 46, 47
Movement of National Conciliation (MCN), 47
Movimiento Anti-Comunista Internacional (MACI), 144
Movimiento por el Socialismo (MPS), 89
Mulattos, 56, 57–58
Municipalities *(municipios)*, 79–80
Muñoz Marín, Luis, 32, 124
Museo del Hombre Dominicano (Museum of Dominican Man), 6

Napoleon Bonaparte, 18
Napoleonic Code, 18, 78
National Assembly, 78
National Businessmen's Council (Consejo Nacional de Hombres de Empresa—CNHE), 94
National Civic Union (UCN), 30–31, 45
National Confederation of Free Laborers (CONATRAL), 35, 95–96, 117
National District, 77, 80
National Federation of Farmers' Brotherhoods (FENHERCA), 98
Nationalism, 109, 111–112, 114
National Police, 33, 102, 104, 130, 131, 137
Neiba Valley, 4
Nicaragua, 22
Nickel, 64, 66, 69
Nineteenth of May group, 104, 131
Nivar Seijas, Neit, 49, 53, 104, 105, 130
Nixon, Richard M., 118

Orfila, Alejandro, 128
Organization of American States (OAS), 28, 38, 39, 40, 42, 52, 112, 120, 121, 123, 125, 126–128
Organized labor, 95–98
Orlich, Francisco, 124
Ortega, Daniel, 124
Ovando, Nicolas de, 15, 16

Panama, 22, 119
Partido Dominicano (PD), 26
Patronage, 77
Peasant movements, 98
Peña Gómez, José Francisco, 37, 51, 53–54, 80, 82–84, 123, 124, 135, 145, 146, 148, 149
Pérez y Pérez, Enrique, 49, 104, 105–106, 131
Philip Morris, 69
Philippines, 22, 23

INDEX

Pigs, 72
Political parties, 81–91, 117
  Dominican Liberation party (PLD), 51, 87–89
  Dominican Revolutionary party (PRD). *See* Dominican Revolutionary party
  minor parties, 89–91
  Popular Democratic party (PDP), 51
  Reformist Social Christian party (PRSC), 84–87, 99, 148
  Social Christian Revolutonary party (PRSC), 37, 40, 45–46, 47, 84–87, 148–149
Population characteristics, 1, 3, 4
  composition, 55
  size, 61
Poverty, 58–61
PRD. *See* Dominican Revolutionary party (PRD)
Provincial government, 79–80
PR (Reformist party), 40, 45, 47, 84, 85
PRSC (Reformist Social Christian party), 84–87, 99, 148
PRSC (Social Christian Revolutionary party), 37, 40, 45–46, 47, 84–87, 148–149
Public transportation system, 133
Public works
  under Balaguer, 44
  under Jorge Blanco, 138, 141
  under Trujillo, 27
  in the United States occupation of 1916 to 1924, 22
Puerto Plata, 4, 64
Puerto Rico, 22, 30, 31, 34

Quisqueyan Democratic party (PQD), 45

Race
  lower classes and, 58
  middle class and, 57–58
  Spanish descendents, 55–56
Radical Revolutionary University Front (FURR), 101
Rafael Abindaer, José, 89
Reagan, Ronald, 115, 140
Red party, 20
Reformist party (Partido Reformista—PR), 40, 45, 47, 84, 85
Reformist Social Christian party (PRSC), 84–87, 99, 148
Reid Cabral, Donald, 36, 37
Repartimiento, 16
Republic of Gran Colombia, 18
Resorts, 4, 6, 67
Ricardo, Joaquín, 86, 146
Rice, 71–72
Rivera Caminero, Francisco, 130
Rivera de Payabo, 70–73

Rockefeller, Nelson, 46
Rodriguez Echavarría, Pedro Santiago, 30, 36
Roosevelt, Theodore, 114
Roosevelt Corollary, 113
Rosario Dominicana S.A., 134
Rosario Sánchez, Francisco del, 19
Ruiz Tejada, Ramón, 47

Saint-Domingue, 17
  slave revolt of 1791 in, 17–18. *See also* Haiti
Samana Bay,14, 20
San Domingo Improvement Company, 21
Santana, Pedro, 19, 20, 110
Santiago, 4
  as cultural capital, 56
  population of, 61
Santiago de los Caballeros, 17
Santo Domingo
  Constitutionalist revolt and, 38–39, 59, 96, 99, 103, 117–118, 128
  Cuban refugees in, 56
  founding of, 15–17
  population of, 61
  poverty in, 58–59
  strike of 1985 in, 143
  tourist industry and, 3, 6, 64
Santos, Emilio de los, 36
Schweitzer, Robert L., 136
Slaves, 15, 16
  abolition of slavery, 18
  revolt of 1791 and, 17–18
Social Christian Revolutionary party (PRSC), 37, 40, 45–46, 47, 84–87, 148–149
Social class, 55
  middle sector, 57–58
  new economic elites, 56–57, 93–94
  poor majority, 58–61, 144, 145
Socialist International, 123, 124
Soviet Union, 112, 114, 128
Spain, 131
  attempted annexation by, 19–20
  cession of Hispaniola to France, 7–8
  colonial period and, 14–17
  descendents of settlers from, 55–56
  discovery of Hispaniola by, 13–15
  expulsion of, 8
Spanish American War, 22, 113
Stevenson, Adlai, 33
Students, 101–102
Sugar, 3, 4–6, 68, 69
  economic dependency on, 62–63
  Gulf and Western Corporation and, 9–10
  land registration act of 1920 and, 23

Tainos, 13–14
Tariff act of 1920, 23

Tavares, Manuel, 148
Taxes
  economic imbalances and, 65
  relief for corporate, 70
  tax-free zones, 66, 67
Tourist industry, 3–7
  growth of, 64–65, 94
Toussaint L'Ouverture, 18
Treaty of Ryswick, 17
Trinitaria, La (The Trinitarian), 19
Triumvirate, 35–37, 40, 44, 50, 103, 121, 125
Trujillo, Rafael, 24, 25–28, 29–30, 42, 63, 71, 85, 90, 93, 111, 147
  armed forces and, 102–103, 119
  assassination of, 28, 29
  Catholic Church and, 98–99
  Haiti and, 119, 120
  middle class under, 57
  new elites under, 56
  Organization of American States and, 26–127
  relations with Latin America and, 123
  United States and, 27–28, 111–112, 116
Trujillo, Ramfis, 29–30, 148

UCN (National Civic Union), 30–31
Unemployment, 58, 60, 65, 70, 77, 97, 132, 143, 150
Union Nacional Dominicana, 25
Union Patriotica (UPA), 89
United Nations, 112, 121, 128
United States
  Balaguer and, 40–42, 43–44
  Bosch government and, 32–35
  customs agreement of 1905 and, 21, 111, 116
  debt and, 21, 110–111
  Dominican role in history of, 114–119
  Guzmán and, 135–136
  Jorge Blanco and, 139–140
  military intervention of 1965 to 1966 and, 8, 109
  occupation by, 8, 21–24, 41–42, 113, 116, 117–118
  relations with, 111–114, 122–123
  Trujillo and, 27–28, 29, 111–112, 116

U.S. Marines, 24–25, 41, 42
U.S. Securities and Exchange Commission (SEC), 67–68
USAID, 118–119

Valdez Hilario, Rafael Adriano, 131, 136
Vásques, Horacio, 25, 26
Vega Real (Royal Plain), 4
Venezuela, 28
Vicente Sanchez, 148
Villeda Morales, Ramon, 124
Viñas Roman, 34, 37
Vinicio Castillo, Marino, 36, 44, 90–91, 146
Volman, Sacha, 32–33, 34, 35, 117

Wessin y Wessin, Elías, 34, 37–38, 45–46, 47, 48, 50, 89, 103
Wheeler, Wayne, 107
Wilson, Woodrow, 21, 22, 25, 114
Women, 23, 79
World Bank, 128
World War I, 22
World War II, 27, 112

Yaque del Norte River, 4
Yost, Robert L., 53